PULSE / IMPULSE

THE ART OF

ROBERT BEHRENS

Gary Dwyer - Editor

Published by Angstrom Unit Works

Text Copyright © 2012 Gary Dwyer. All rights reserved.
Photographs unless otherwise noted, © 2012 Estate of Robert Behrens

No Part of this book may be reproduced or transmitted in any form
by any means, electronic or mechanical, including photocopying, recording,
or by any information storage or retrieval system without written permission
from the publisher, except for the inclusion of brief quotations in a review.

This book was composed using: LeArchitect, Univers LT std and Minion Pro.

Warning and Disclaimer
This book is designed to provide information to photographers, curators, arts administrators and students
Every effort has been made to make this book complete and accurate as possible,
but no warranty of fitness is implied.

The information is provided on an as-is basis. The author and publisher shall have neither
liability nor responsibility to any person or entity with respect to any loss or damages arising
from the information contained in this book.

ISBN 978-0-9849639-3-5

Cover Photograph: Pulse / Impulse drawing © 2012 Estate of Robert Behrens

Further information about the editor is available on the web:
garydwyerphotography.com

Purpose

This book is dedicated to the memory of Robert Behrens.

Let's start this out by saying I am not a biographer, I am only trying not to forget a great friend. Even so, I have all the problems of a real biographer. Along with what is included here there are many missing pieces, wrong dates, misstated facts, ignorance, and ocassionally I have been oblivious to what others would see as obvious truths. And I ask forgiveness for these faults.

I have included almost no mention of Robert's personal relationships and this is intentional. It is to protect the living. Their stories are profound and I don't want to get any aspect of those stories wrong. I know a lot of anecdotal stories my own about Robert, but I really know little outside our friendship and what I saw in his work.

Individuals who have made substantial contributions to this project are Gaeta Stratton
Marga Friberg, Peter Conrad Tea and Faye Behrens. Individual photographic contributions are attributed adjacent to the images.

Robert Behrens

1939 - 2008

Denver Technological Center
H$_2$0 Works 1971

Pueblo, Colorado circa 1971

My name is Robert Behrens.

I have worked as an environmental sculptor since I graduated from University of Denver in 1968. My love has been to create beautiful spaces through sculpture, landscape or architecture.

I have always worked in sculpture in the public realm. Most all of my work is rooted both psychologically and physically in its place. My pieces can't be moved. Many have foundations underground almost as large as the sculpture which is seen. The first period of my work was in wood, large pressure treated wood. The second period was in steel. These steel pieces often were then covered with diffraction grading, a mylar that diffracts sunlight into spectral light. The colors change as the observer changes location. This makes every viewers experience unique. Most of my work is additive, smaller pieces of material combined in space to make a whole.

Over many years, through my own work and through the collaborations that I have done with G Cabell Childress, Architect, I have observed that there are different scales of sculpture. For each individual piece to be successful, it must address the scale of the physical place and the pace of the people who inhabit that space.

Scale 1; Intimate, the art can be small, the spaces which the artwork inhabits are smaller either by their physical nature, by the density of people or from the slowness of speed which people move through the space. The distance from the observer to the artwork is small and the observer can recognize, be detained and take time to contemplate the emotional experience conveyed through the piece of work.

Scale 2: Architectural : The artwork can respond to a space formed by the interior or the exterior of buildings or walls. The work, by its confirmation, can make the observer or a person moving through a space more aware of their own movement and in doing so bring an observer into the experience of a work of art. The volume formed by the space itself is more defined and enhanced by the successful artwork.

Scale 3; Monumental, An artwork becomes the landmark for a point in space. The physical environs can be large, even a landscape. To be successful at this scale a piece must be large enough to be read from a distance and focus the observer's energy. The artwork makes a focus in itself and makes a statement as to a point in space.

My work is in Scale 2 and 3.

My hope is that seeing my work will inspire other sculptors to think about public art works and how they influence the lives of all those who move and work around those pieces. Our cities and cultures are only as great as those places of beauty that survive the individual.

I wish everyone peace and beauty. Robert Behrens

Pueblo, Colorado circa 1971

University of Denver Denver, Colorado 1972

Wood Construction, Denver Art Museum
Denver, Colorado 1972

Denver Art Museum, Denver, Colorado

At 2 AM the phone rang.

It was Robert, and he said, "I've got all the streets blocked off with police cars and a crane with my five-ton sculpture dangling from the hook. The problem is that we can't stop it from spinning around and if we just set it down it will break in half. (slight pause) You're the only guy I know that can figure this out, has a welding truck and will come down to the museum in the middle of the night to do a little steel work." I said, "Keep, those police lights flashing, I'll be there in twenty minutes."

-Gary Dwyer

Before we go any further we have to get a few things straight...

Artists lives in America are usually astoundingly difficult. Particularly visual artists. Occasionally glamorous on the outside, but on the inside filled with unstable relationships, confusion and angst. If an artist decides to make Public Art, then they are saddled with clients' aspirations, building codes and an almost unimaginable morass of problems never confronted by any artists who work only in their studio.

Robert and I grew up in an era when we thought art could change the world. It turns out that art can only change is the artist. After having completed twenty-five years of sculpture on three continents I can say that Public Art is a particularly malodorous place to play. It rumbles around in the regions between deception and despair, and later, the neglect of the work, even destruction or disappearance occurs. It is no place for dilettantes.

I first met Robert Behrens in 1969 on the first day of Graduate School at the University of Denver. We were two of three students enrolled for Master's degrees in sculpture. The facilities for making sculpture at the University were pathetic and I think that one of the reasons I was admitted to the program was that I had my own studio. It was a beat up garage / barn with a dirt floor on the outskirts of Denver, but at least it was something the University didn't have to provide.

Robert had his own studio too. It was adjacent to his home in rural Evergreen. He had built both his home and the studio. Either that or made major renovations so it was visible that a modernist architect had come to the mountains of Colorado, even if it was via New Jersey, Kansas City, and numerous other places.

The third sculptor in our group was A. Thomas Schomberg. The following clip from his web site should give an indication of his very creative life:

"The sculpture career of A. Thomas Schomberg has spanned the last four decades of creativity in which Schomberg has described, with his realistic intensity, the time and environment in which he lives and the society that we are all captives of.

Schomberg grew up in America's Midwest - Iowa during the 1940's and 50's. After studying for a short time in Europe and completing an M.F.A. (master of fine arts) degree, plus additional post graduate study, Schomberg then moved to the east coast and taught for four years in a progressive community college. Though he received tenure, he felt compelled to relocate to Colorado in 1975 and establish Schomberg studios. Since then, Schomberg and his wife, Cynthia, who is also his agent, have worked together to pursue Schomberg's career as a professional sculptor. Several years later and after countless exhibits, Schomberg established a strong client base. Numbered among these clients and collectors are blue collar workers, entrepreneurs, museum directors/curators, professional athletes and movie stars, including Sylvester Stallone. Stallone went on to Select Schomberg to create what was later to become the iconic ROCKY statue for the movie, 'Rocky I I I'.
http://www.schombergstudios.com/

The three of us were graduate teaching assistants and taught first year basic design. Because all of us had some prior teaching experience we were pretty much left alone, to our own devices, and so much so that Robert and I decided to team-teach. The classes were in an old post office that had been divided into two big rooms.
Robert and I decided it would be better if there were one big room, so we worked with the students to cut a sixteen-foot diameter hole in the dividing wall.

The administration was not pleased with our activities, but since we were saving the University a piles of money by teaching many classes, we had quite a lot of latitude. We had almost no guidance or mentoring. Being left alone meant we spent a lot of time together talking about our own work as artists and what was going on in the art world. We also spent a lot of time reading art magazines from New York and agonizing about Denver being a kind of cultural backwater at the time.

Tom Schomberg came to get his Master's degree in sculpture because he wanted to be a sculptor.

I had come to attempt a Master's in sculpture because I wanted to teach at the university level and to make a bridge between landscape architecture and sculpture. Robert's background in architecture had many similarities to mine and consequently we hit it off right away.

All architects want to be sculptors, but Robert was the only sculptor I ever met who wanted to be an architect. Many of his projects are that very sophisticated and ill-defined space between urban design, landscape architecture and large scale sculpture. He was as interested in making spaces and experiences as he was in making objects. He had the architect's fanaticism about detail while always having an eye out for how to make the project bigger, to have more influence, to engage a wider audience.

Of the three of us, Robert had established the most consistent form language. A signature of rectangular members rotated in space. Tom, on the other hand, was obviously trained classically and had a profound interest in the human form but was working in many directions at the time, serious social commentary pervading many of his efforts.

My thesis project was for the central campus plaza of Colorado Academy and led to my collaboration with Robert on an 'Art as Urban Design' project for the City of Littleton, Colorado.

Robert always wanted to be something other than what he was. He wanted to be an architect, but refused to accept the responsibility and drudgery and hierarchy that went along with it.

He wanted to be a collaborator on everything, but his ego always got in his way and got in everyone else's way too. He disliked my need for security and my ability to vfind stable jobs at various universities but he envied the guaranteed salary they brought. He dreamed of a "cushy" professorship that would free him to make his own sculpture, but he never wanted to do all the ass kissing and loop jumping that come along with those not-so-cushy University jobs.

Robert was a geometry and symmetry freak. He was educated during the modernist period and design was simply modernist dogma. Robert thought he was an original, singular, one-off. I never remember him speaking of influences. Of course he knew about Larry Bell and George Rickey and Mies van der Rohe and all the Bauhaus geniuses, but somehow he didn't seem to think they had any effect on him. These people might have been in his brain, but he never seemed to bow in the direction or Kenneth Snelson or James Turrell.

Dale Eldred, at the Kansas City Art Institute, was the single most powerful influence in Robert's artistic life. Robert gave him homage all the time.

< en.wikipedia.org/wiki/Dale_Eldred >
http://168.144.121.83/culturereport/artists/eldred/index.htm

Robert loved to build models of his projects and he could see himself walking through the spaces he created. He always wanted to have things line up. Rectangles were a big deal. Euclidian geometry and Newtonian physics ruled Robert's world. It was the revenge of modernism and contemporary materials used at an architectural scale. He couldn't be a stone carver if it would save his life.

He demanded industrial perfection in everything he did, and could not tolerate anything but excellence from those he worked with. He often used his soft voice and gharming smile to be demanding. And - yes - He could be a royal pain in the ass.

But with the smile and the voicehe usually got people to see things his way. I miss his voice and his smile. I miss him.

- Gary Dwyer

GOING, GOING--GONE

By Michael Paglia in WESTWORD - Denver published: September 27, 1995 (Exerpt)

Lately, and increasingly, museums across the country and around the world have begun "deaccessioning"--selling off parts of their existing collections as a ready source of "free money" to pay for new acquisitions. It's money, more than art, that's hard for many of these institutions to come by, especially in recent years, as private and public funding sources have dried up right and left. So it's easy to understand the temptation for museum directors to clean out their storerooms and cash in. Not to be left out, the Denver Art Museum is currently in the midst of an unprecedented deaccession campaign, which reached a kind of crescendo with the September 16 on-premises auction conducted by the prominent New York-based Christie's auction house. At the all-day event, DAM divested itself of some 1,500 articles sold in more than 600 lots.

Even under ideal circumstances--which this was--the process of getting rid of once-treasured works of art is filled with pitfalls. It does break a faith with donors. And it comes with a checkered history: Scandal, or at least controversy, has accompanied deaccessioning efforts more often than not in the museum world... One deaccession decision made by the museum inadvertently puts the institution square in the middle of another debate--this one over the place of public art in our city. Almost from the 1971 opening of DAM's current home--the distinctive building designed by Gio Ponti and James Sudler--the corner in front of the museum was marked by a large minimalist sculpture, "Untitled (Environmental Fan Sculpture)," by Robert Behrens, an artist who worked briefly in Denver. The sculpture was commissioned by the museum for the site, but because Behrens donated his time, DAM only sprang for the cost of materials. It's understandable why this piece sold to a prominent local collector for just $1,380--few people would have the space to display the piece, which is the size of a small house. Today, in place of the fan sculpture, is a garden installation by Meg Webster. This is progress?

One thing the DAM presumably wouldn't get rid of, if it had the choice, is the 1981 "Solar Fountain," by internationally known artists Larry Bell and Eric Orr, which sits on the barren lawn of the Denver Center for the Performing Arts. But the DCPA, unlike the museum, hasn't yet reached the point of being professionally organized, and there the director calls all the shots. That enthusiastic (and autocratic) amateur, Donald Seawell, is not so careful about such things, and he's decided the fountain must go.

As a result, the fountain, which has already been sold down the river by the kangaroo Mayor's Commission on Art, Culture and Film will surely soon be gone, to be replaced by a park. The only person with the power to grant it a reprieve is Mayor Wellington Webb. It is to laugh.

The passing of the fountain may not be mourned by more than a few, but it's hardly an artistic embarrassment. Its style is completely compatible with the DCPA buildings. And if this example of solar art never quite worked as it was supposed to, neither did solar energy. The disappearance of both the fan sculpture and the fountain makes one wonder if any public art in Denver from the 1970s or 1980s will manage to survive into the next century. Most likely not--though much of the city's more recent public art, with more questionable credentials than the older stuff, probably will. It's doubly sad that the official disregard for Colorado art exemplified by the DAM auction extends even to works by out-of-towners that had the bad fortune to wind up here. The best example of that comes not from the world of art but from architecture: the pending destruction of I.M. Pei's Zeckendorf Plaza.

Oh, well. Denver has never been known for its important public art or architecture. Given current events, it never will be.

Even though both Robert and I had experience in urban design and architecture, it was in the realm of sculpture that we felt most comfortable. The problem is that we really liked working on extremely big sculpture projects.

The then small town of Littleton Colorado was interested in re-vitalizing its image and contacted Robert and myself to determine if revitalization was possible by the town becoming known for its art collection. Not by what they had in a gallery of museum, but what they had on the streets and sidewalks. This was before the idea of "Public Art Programs" had become common and seemed a novel idea worth investigating.

The scale of the endeavor was unlimited and it was possible to make suggestions for vast changes and minor improvements. The real goal was to use art to put the town back on the map.

I say back on the map because it was once an important grain milling town attending to the needs of the farmers in the region, but like many if not all American river towns, there was a significant period when these towns turned their backs on the very rivers that caused the towns to come into existence. Much of it was connected to the rise of the railroads and truck transport, but it wasn't until well after Cleveland's Cuyahoga river caught on fire in 1969 that we began to change the relationship between our rivers and towns. Suggesting sculptures to be placed on the sidewalks was not going to solve this problem, nor was it going to make the town into an art Mecca for tourists.

This was originally published in the 2007 book "Context" By Gary Dwyer

-Gary Dwyer

river edge fjord system

The most vexing problem of towns adjacent to rivers and streams is what to do in or on the floodplain. In this case, The Army Corps of Engineers said it would cost 14 Million dollars (1971) to channelize (i.e. pave) that portion of the floodplain most likely to flood the town. Our proposal was to take the fourteen million dollars and buy the floodplain and turn it into a park. Any flooding would cause very minimal damage to any structures.

(Our design for the park was not accomplished, but I understand the floodplain was purchased. Years later I learned the same idea was accomplished in Canberra, Australia.)

steam jets in river

During the last fifty years, substantial manufacturing plants located nearby needed to periodically discharge waste steam. We thought this would ad visual interest to the river until we realized this would raise the temperature of the river and damage the habitat. However we also discovered it was necessary to periodically bleed the compressed air tanks at several plants and the installation of a series of pipes in the river bottom could provide a kind of air fountain and actually improve the water quality through the added oxygenation.

spherical floatables

The primary component in visibility is contrast and the best way to make someone see something is by having something where it doesn't belong. The bow-tie on the dog system. As it nears Denver, the South Platte is normally a brown river. Raging in the spring and mild mannered in the fall, but almost always brown. The Addition of bright colors and movement would go a long way to increasing awareness that the river was actually a vibrant and important part of the community.

The largest forms constructed for the least amount of money are made of earth. Dirt has certain gravitational rules, but retaining walls are very inexpensive and are very cost effective. Landscape as play equipment. Note to the art history savvy: This design was produced before any of the earthworks of people like Herbert Bayer or Robert Morris.

One of the most hotly debated issues among those concerned with the "quality" of the landscape is whether we should make the highway driving experience as pleasant as possible or we should make it as horrible as possible in order to discourage driving individual cars. No matter which side of this issue you stand, everyone agrees the noise from highways is a negative addition to our communities. Solid masonry is the only thing that stops sound and as cars and trucks will continue to pass through our towns and cities, artists should be hired to design the walls. (See the left side of this image.)

pedestrian underpass

Inevitable conflicts between pedestrians and road and rail traffic are seldom handled with any grace. Most often a pedestrian underpass is to be avoided as a place of darkness, danger and urine. Clean, open and well lit, this example is intended to be reminiscent of the cavernous Colorado mines, but this time, with an opening at the other end.

city gateway

Western towns seldom have any sense of edge or boundary. Particularly those in flatlands and as a consequence, there is often no sense of entry or exit and it is difficult to know very much about where you are. We decided a large earth form cut through by the main road would provide the kind of visual punctuation necessary to announce the entrance to the town.

Littleton, Colorado 1971

Direct interaction with the river was essential to improving the relationship between the river and the town and if we were going to have a pedestrian bridge to solve a circulation problem, it should also be an event, a destination. Going upstream, against the current, contrary to logic, an enormous jet of intermittent water passes over the pedestrian bridge. Yes, some people get wet. You take your chances.

Traffic triangles in America are some of the least developed and most ignored urban spaces. We would do well to look to England and France to see what they have done with many of their roundabouts. This triangle in Denver was a competition instigated by the city in conjunction with the adjacent Cherry Creek Shopping Center. I have no recollection why I was selected for the commission. The basin is eighteen inches deep to conform with public safety code of the time. (1972) Notice the unscripted child in the foreground is running *toward* the water.

Druid's Drinking Fountain
Denver, Colorado 1972-74

This project was designed by Gary Dwyer with **contract documents and construction supervision by Robert Behrens**

The pointy upward bits fountain are a rather obvious reference to the Rockies being this regions' most important source of water. A major consideration in the design of this fountain was the intention to have it left on during the winter so it would freeze and make icicle sculptures. I have visited in winter and it was turned off. I have never seen a photograph to indicate that this has icicle idea has ever happened.

- Gary Dwyer

Editor's note: This article was written in response to the May 7 request of Mayor William McNichols that Robert Behrens' sculpture, Earth Crystal, be removed from its site in front of Currigan Hall, as the City of Denver could not afford its upkeep.

On Wednesday, June 18. just as **'The Muse'** *was being typeset, we learned that the Denver Art Commission had voted to move or destroy the sculpture.*

by Jeffrey C. McCarthy

"The legislature of the State of Colorado has declared 'The State of Colorado, in recognition of its responsibility to create a more humane environment of distinction, enjoyment, and pride for all of its citizen sand in recognition that public art is a resource which stimulates the vitality and economy of the state's communities, finds and declares ... that the general welfare of the people of the state will be promoted by giving further recognition to the arts and humanities as a vital part of our culture and heritage and, as an
important means of expanding the scope of our community life ... that the arts
and humanities in the life of our communities will continue to grow and to
play an even more significant part in the welfare and educational experience of our citizens and to establish the paramount position of this state in the nation and in the world as a cultural center . . ."

The problem is that not everyone got the message. The City and County of Denver is seeking to celebrate its position as a world cultural center by demolishing one of its few pieces of outdoor sculpture.

In 1974, at a cost of approximately $28,000, two-thirds of which was public money, the Denver Parks and Recreation Foundation, Inc. (the Park People) commissioned the design and Construction of the "Earth Crystal," for placement in front of the Currigan Convention Center.

The Earth Crystal was donated and dedicated to the people of the City andCounty of Denver in July, 1975. It was a moving ceremony - the Mayor wasthere, the press was there, the people were there. It seemed almost as if the city's motto with respect to works of art (Qui id petit? qui id reqirit? qui carrit?) was a thing of the past. It wasn't to be. After a time the City began to neglect the piece. The sod died, the earth was washed away, the mirror surface was neither washed nor maintained. The obvious neglect of the piece advertised anopen season for vandals. and they administered the *coup de grace* with Ripple bottles and stones; although it appears that a certain amount of the damage to the glass surface may have been caused by City lawn mowers. The artist filed suit to have the Earth Crystal repaired and properly maintained. But apparently the City would rather have it destroyed.

It has been proven conclusively that objects obviously neglected are extremely
likely to become the targets of vandalism. It is not for aesthetic purposes that the owners of vacant buildings quickly replace broken windows; they are replaced to save the unbroken ones. Some people, however, have charged that the Earth Crystal's problems were created by the artist because the Earth Crystal is not "vandal proof." But what is? Nothing. With the possible exception of NORAD headquarters buried within Cheyenne Mountain. Why should ahigher standard be required of works of art?

Our homes and public buildings are
not designed to be vandal proof or even vandal resistant. There have been no reports of a run on the bullet-proof glass industry. The materials used in the Earth Crystal were more or less the same as, and if anything stronger than, the materials commonly employed in downtown buildings. In any event, the City accepted the piece "as is." It knew what it was getting.

Objects are vandalized. Empty bottle sand cans of spray paint unfortunately have become the tools of expressions of alienation. The real issue is not whether vandalism can be defeated by building vandal proof structures - even if we wished to encase everything in steel and granite - but rather our response once an object has been vandalized.

The City has said that it will cost too much to repair the Earth Crystal. Loosely translated, this means that the piece is not worth the money that it would cost to repair it. Which objects are worthy of repair? Is there any doubt that Bucko the Bronco, perched atop the

Earth Crystal Denver 1974

scoreboard at Mile High stadium, would be repaired if vandalized, no matter the cost? How about the lettering identifying McNichols arena? There are a great many objects which the City would repair even though not absolutely essential to the health and welfare of City residents. Why does the City refuse to repair the Earth Crystal; is art that low on the scale of values and priorities?

It is, of course, a. political decision. The Earth Crystal has no constituency. It ishard to argue with the proposition that there are people and protect in greater need of City money and City attention - it is true. On the other, hand it is not as if public art, including the repair and maintenance of the Earth Crystal, demands an inordinate or disproportionate share of City money and resources. We should be able to spend a modest amount of money on the care and maintenance of public art. The cost is small and the beneficiaries are many.

Other cities have faced the same dilemma. Some cities have acquitted themselves admirably, others haven't. In1977, George Rickey loaned a work of kinetic sculpture to the town of Hoosick Falls, New York. The work was valued at $60,000. According to Rickey, he loaned it "because one shouldn't do things · just for big cities." In 1979, the village trustees voted to get rid of the sculpture unless Rickey paid the sculpture's $333 annual insurance bill. The town was not willing to pay $333 a year for the beauty and joy of the work.

The saga of the Watts Towers in Los Angeles is another matter. In 1921, Simon Rodia, an Italian immigrant, slowly began building the three Watts Towers,the tallest of which eventually reached 100 feet. The labor took 33 years. Asked why he did it. Rodia is reported to have said, "A man has to be good good or bad bad to be remembered." For those who have seen them, the Towers are an awesome monument to one man's artistic determination. After the ailing Rodia abandoned the Towers in 1954, they fell into a state of neglect and disrepair. Demolition was imminent.

In 1959, however, the Nonprofit Committee for Simon Rodia's Towers in Watts· was formed - the Towers had a champion! There insued a 20-year battle between the Committee, the City of Los Angeles and the State of California over whether the Towers should be preserved and, if so, who should pay the bill. To . date, having weathered charges of fanaticism. etc., the committee has won - the Towers have been preserved and are undergoing competent restoration.

What makes this case different from the case of the Earth Crystal? If anything, the Watts Towers are less resistant to vandalism and the elements than the Earth Crystal. Watts has, at times, been a tough neighborhood on outdoor monuments, certainly more demanding than downtown Denver. Perhaps the difference lies in the recognition by the .Watts Committee and ultimately the City of Los Angeles and State of California that the Watts

Towers are worthy of preservation, that preservation costs money and that the money should be spent. There is another difference. The Watts Towers found. a champion. For 20 years the committee worked unceasingly to preserve both the existence and integrity of the Towers. No one in Denver has taken on that role with respect to the Earth Crystal or any other work of City-owned public art. The Park People have boon strangely quiet and unsympathetic. The burden of protecting the Earth Crystal has, by default, been left to the artist.

It is an issue of values. We may not be concerned with the probable findings of 22nd Century archaeologists to the effect that we had great storm drains but not culture. But we might be more concerned with our vision of our environment, an environment which is often inhuman and out-of-scale. The history of urban dwelling is a chronicle of the inch-by-inch erosion of human scale. The Earth Crystal seems oddly out of place in its bigger than life environment. It is a reminder that there is something else. It is a reminder that our environment can be humanized.

Aside from the fact that it would be an unwarranted breach of faith with the taxpayers and private contributors who paid for the piece to do otherwise, the Earth Crystal should be restored and maintained. We can choose our monuments.

Earth Crystal Denver 1974

METRO NEWS

THE DENVER POST Wed., Oct. 8, 1980 25 SECTION B

Artist Victorious: 'Earth Crystal' To Be Restored

By BOB THRELKELD
Denver Post Staff Writer

In a victory for Denver artist Robert Behrens, city officials have agreed to restore and properly maintain the deteriorated "Earth Crystal" sculpture in front of Currigan Hall.

Behrens sued the city last year claiming his $28,000 mirrored-glass sculpture had been altered and damaged through poor maintenance and vandalism. He claimed an artist had a right to demand his work be properly preserved even after it no longer belonged to him.

The sculpture was donated to the city in 1975 by The Park People, a private organization which works closely with the city's art commission and Parks Department.

Mayor Bill McNichols originally praised the donation, but later tried to have it removed and given to a private contractor for placement in a business park. The arts commission last June conceded the sculpture was "something of an embarassment because of its condition," but refused to allow the city to remove the sculpture.

City Attorney Max Zall said Tuesday the city will pay $10,000 to restore and maintain the sculpture if the Park People also raises $10,000.

The out-of-court settlement also acknowledges the city's "moral responsibility" to properly maintain and care for public art and preserve it in its original form.

Behrens' attorney, Jeffery McCarthy, said the settlement "achieved everything that we set out to do without going to trial." McCarthy called it a "reasonable solution to the problem."

Since Behrens' suit was filed in March 1979, the city has moved to prevent similar problems with donated artwork in the future. The City Council has approved an ordinance allowing city officials to require cash deposits from donors to cover the possible repair or rehabilitation of the artwork.

Denver Post Photo
MIRRORED SCULPTURE HAS BEEN CENTER OF CONTROVERSY
City officials have agreed to protect the sculpture from vandalism.

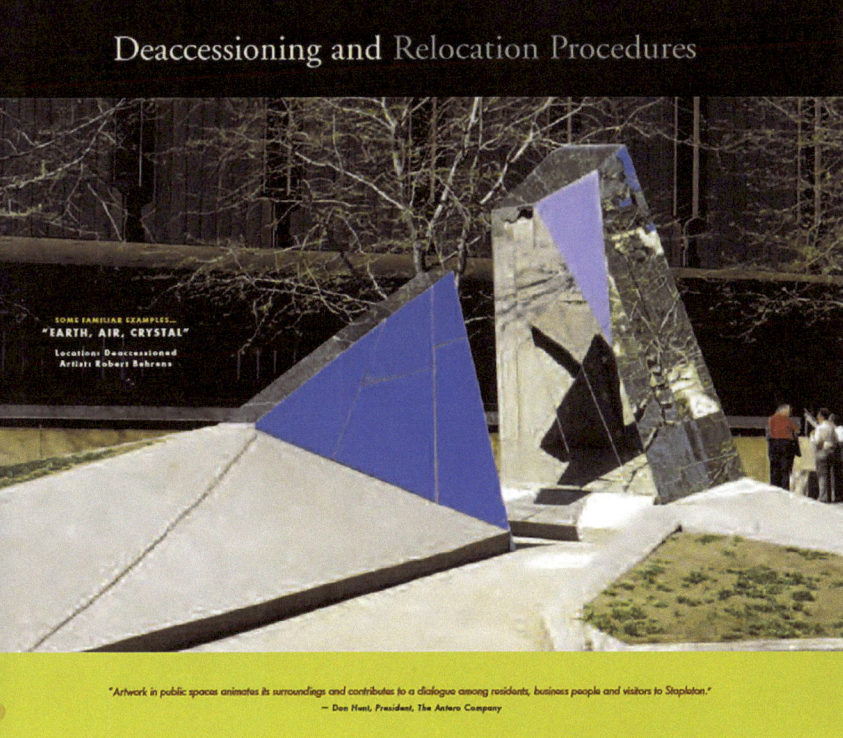

Robert Behrens' 'Earth Crystal.'

'Earth Crystal' reflects Denver sights

Working in a little-used medium for sculpture—glass—Colorado artist Robert Behrens has created "Earth Crystal" for the plaza of the Denver Convention Center. The work consists of two elements, the highest 15 ft, and was commissioned by the Park People Inc. program of Denver funded through the National Endowment for the Arts. By day or night the 12 mirrored facets reflect the changing environment. The sculpture is self-supporting with no interior framework. Behrens studied architecture at Pratt Institute and later received degrees in fine arts; he works from a studio in Conifer, CO. Construction/design collaborator was Frank Seiburth.

Progressive Architecture
July 1977 A Penton/IPC Reinhold Publication

Picnic Shelters   Cherry Creek Reservoir, Colorado 1975

Picnic Shelters
Cherry Creek Reservoir, Colorado 1975

Bold forms establish a sense of place in "wide-open" spaces

As opposed to the "background" structures of stone and timber often commissioned for large parks devoted to active recreation, these three isolated groups of structures—by their individual visual strengths—establish reference points in the vast open landscape of the Cherry Creek Reservoir near Denver. Designed by architects Cabell Childress Associates, they create sophisticated though differing images; the buildings, by their arrangement, contain small "urban" spaces. And all of this is appropriate to the site and forms an "extension" of the ambiance of the urban center that touches the park's border. There was a limited budget, and another constraint was the structures' ability to withstand periodic flooding. Perhaps most importantly, the Cherry Creek structures represent a breakthrough for design commissioned by local government; besides winning A.I.A. awards, the picnic shelters (photo, right top) and the marina (photos, right) were displayed as "desirable solutions" at a 1974 Colorado Design Assembly sponsored by the Governor.

The marina's full budget of $67,000 was to include a clear indication to distant boats of its purpose: home base. The architect's answer was two identifying concrete "sails in full wind" painted bright orange.

To produce the "flying wing" shapes of the concrete picnic shelters, the architects worked with sculptor Robert Behrens. The flaring roofs each shelter two tables from sun and rain, and give identity to a strip of relatively featureless shore line. The formwork was made from 3- by 6-inch timbers threaded together on pipe, and the optimum number for one form's use (10) dictated the number of structures currently in place. At the beach facility, the low buildings produce contained outdoor spaces.

CHERRY CREEK MARINA, Denver, Colorado. Owner: *Colorado Department of Parks*. Architects: *Cabell Childress and Martha Russell*. Structural engineer: *Borman & Melcher*. General contractor: *Hyder Construction Co.*
CHERRY CREEK PICNIC SHELTERS, Denver, Colorado. Owner: *Colorado Department of Parks*. Architects: *Cabell Childress*. Sculptor: *Robert Behrens*. Structural engineers: *KKBNA*. General contractor: *Blackinton & Decker*.
CHERRY CREEK BEACH FACILITIES, Denver, Colorado. Owner: *Colorado Department of Parks*. Architects: *Cabell Childress*. Engineers: KKBNA (structural); *McFall & Konkel* (mechanical); Sol Flax (electrical). Contractor: Connor Construction Co.

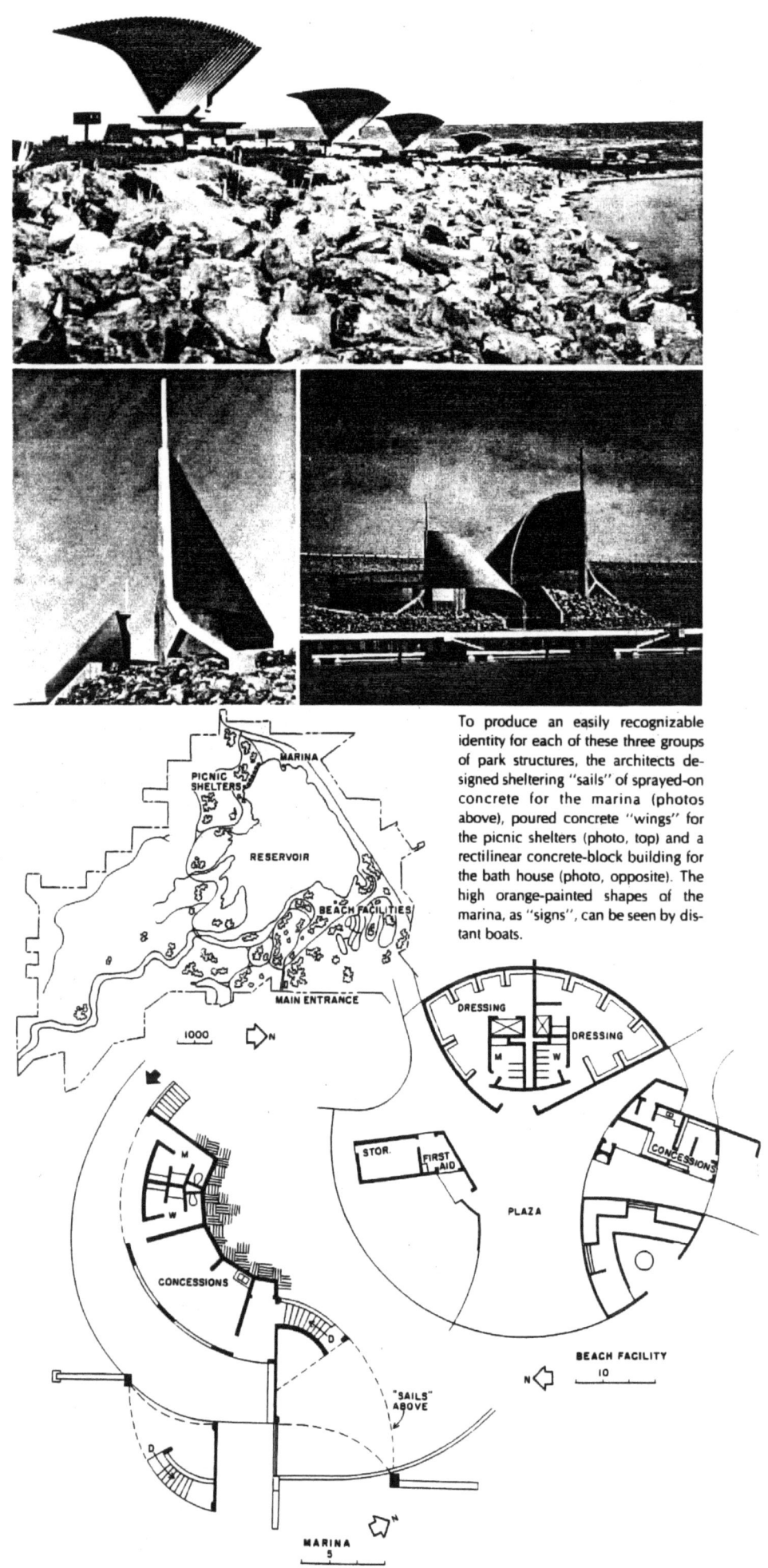

To produce an easily recognizable identity for each of these three groups of park structures, the architects designed sheltering "sails" of sprayed-on concrete for the marina (photos above), poured concrete "wings" for the picnic shelters (photo, top) and a rectilinear concrete-block building for the bath house (photo, opposite). The high orange-painted shapes of the marina, as "signs", can be seen by distant boats.

Picnic Shelters
Cherry Creek Reservoir, Colorado 1975

Standing Wave
Vancouver, British Columbia 1977

From the Capilano Review – Vancouver 1977

Robert Behrens / STANDING WAVE

"I work in different materials-~ steel, concrete, glass and wood. Wood is a problem when you're using it in any condition where the climate changes, where the sun's up on one side and down on the other, or if it's in a dry condition then a moist condition. The material moves constantly in and out, so I've taken precautions in that regard. Standing Wave is under such a tremendous amount of compression that any small amount of shrinkage or expansion is not going to affect it. The pressure treatment tends to reduce the possibility of the sculpture taking on moisture or losing moisture, so it's going to be quite stable. The piece is constructed from 3 x 12 hemlock pieces- 4-0 pieces of 20 foot lengths, the remaining pieces in 8 foot lengths, all threaded about a 6 inch pipe. They're each fastened to the next one, continuously. I moved them as they were being placed. The pipe has a threaded rod that goes through the en tire piece, and between the pipe and the rod there's gravel. When all the pieces were placed, then a nut was put on each end of the threaded rod and a hydraulic jack compressed the entire thing together - it's" post-tension construction.

I think that the siting of the work comes down to an understanding of the element of designs in space- a concept that goes back to the Renaissance tradition and even before that. Sculpture is not just an object to be seen in a gallery; it's something that has play and interplay with the people in the place where it's located. The Ambleside site we eventually agreed to is great. It gave me the chance to do a piece of sculpture that was similar to my original design, but which related more intimately to the idea of being near the water, a kind of wave form.

I wanted to make for Vancouver a sculpture that embodied the idea of things that go in and out, the coming and going of a harbour, the idea of departure, the frame in which departure happens. It also, hopefully, gives a symbolic sense of arrival. Since I'm from the interior of the continent, it was for me very exciting and important to recognize where the water is and I wanted my sculpture to be near the water.

What I'm always doing with my sculpture is to make something where the work is in visual harmony with what is happening in the place. I like to make a clear statement of intent, so my work is simplified. By simplification I mean that I search for a common denominator- some place for the sculpture to happen. I see the wood method I use as a natural process because I take pieces of material without essentially altering them.

I take them the way they come from the manufacturer without altering dimension, drill a few holes in each one, put the pieces together. The sculpture is made out of right angles - flat surfaces that are put together and come out as something curved, something soft.

The artist has the opportunity of removing himself from the industrial process in a certain way; the artist can observe what industry can produce which strikes in him a chord of harmony. My interest is in finding a process so simple, so direct that the result of that process is actually the summation of all the bits and pieces it takes to get there, something that's entirely greater than any bit or part of the process."

Light Stripes - Colorado circa 1980

Light Cathedral, Colorado circa 1980

Light Lines, Denver 1980

Crystal Entry, Denver circa 1980

Lifescape Fountain
Denver circa 1980

Bob Behrens, *Arcade*, 30' × 153' wood, 1981.

BOB BEHRENS
at Inkfish, Denver

Integrating art with life is a lofty ambition, and one which is not at all common even among artists. For Bob Behrens, it has been a pursuit throughout his career. From the moment of entry into his exhibit "Wood: Revolutions of Scale" at Inkfish Gallery, one is struck by the realization that this is not merely a retrospective. Behrens has availed himself of the opportunity to utilize the entire space of the gallery, and thus has created a new environment which is part gallery and part sculpture. The whole is an exciting visual experience that is greater than the sum of its parts.

His approach to exhibiting his pieces, done over the past 12 years, involved channeling the viewer through the gallery. Although Inkfish is a small, cubical space, through the addition of a constructed black wall, and a double large-scale sculpture, the gallery is transformed to a luxuriant ambience. The viewer, of necessity, is participatory and, traveling through space, experiences a heightened involvement with the individual pieces. The works themselves are displayed in a variety of forms which encompass several modes of expression. The exhibit includes photographs of existing sculptures, small wood models, a site analysis for an upcoming large piece and is dominated by two large pieces built specifically for the show. The variety of expressive forms suggests a Renaissance versatility.

The re-designing of the gallery is an exciting approach to the context of total design. The strength of the show, however, is not limited to this melding of different approaches. As a retrospective exhibit, it is only natural to compare and contrast the early pieces with the recent. Behrens has received several large commissions over the past 12 years, so several of the early works are well-known at their original sites as well as through photographic reproduction. Representative of the early mode is the large fan-shaped wood sculpture situated in front of the Denver Art Museum. Whereas this piece is potentially powerful—it is held together under extreme tension—the power is never obvious on a visual level. On the contrary, the appearance is placid; there is a divergence between concept and actuality.

Although Behrens' recent sculptures and models in wood bear some resemblance to the Denver Art Museum piece, they have taken an important step beyond their predecessors. Several years ago, a trip to Italy influenced his art vocabulary and appears to be responsible for this exciting new turn in his work. *Arcade*, a small model in wood, is the direct translation of this experience. This piece resembles his early fan-shaped pieces but adds another twist in axis and, rather than being at eye level with the viewer, it is modelled to loom overhead as an environmental passageway. This Renaissance influence has become the important fulcrum for Behrens' work. The two large, wooden sculptures, one that acts as a sentinel and preview outside the gallery and the double *Forest I & II* carry the vitality of *Arcade* to a larger scale.

"Wood: Revolutions of Scale" signals a new direction in the already full career of Bob Behrens. There is a continuity to the work that spans 23 years, but the recent surge of ideas provides anticipation for the growth and development of his environmental approach to public sculpture and signals a further integration of art and life.

—Carol Maus

Bob Behrens, *Forest I & II*, 9'6" x 16" x 7'4" wood.

Bob Behrens, *Untitled* (Denver Art Museum). 18' x 28' x 28' wood.

Line Fragments, University of Colorado, Boulder, 1981

Colorado Daily

Vol. 29 No. 349 · Wednesday/Thursday - July 8-9, 1981 · FREE

First woman appointed to the Supreme Court

ERA, abortion foes promise battle

WASHINGTON (UPI) — President Reagan, in an appointment he said would be "one of the proudest legacies of my presidency," announced Tuesday he will nominate Arizona state Judge Sandra O'Connor as the first woman on the Supreme Court.

Reagan called the 51-year-old O'Connor, who would replace Potter Stewart and break a tradition going back to George Washington, "a person for all seasons."

First reaction from the Senate indicated she could have an easy time being confirmed by the Senate, although opponents of the Equal Rights Amendment and abortion immediately promised to battle the nomination, holding Reagan's feet to the fire on anti-abortion language in the 1980 Republican platform.

"We are astounded at what has occurred — that the first woman appointed to the U.S. Supreme Court, although competent and articulate, has a pro-abortion voting record in the years 1970 through 1974 in the Arizona state Senate," said Dr. Carolyn Gerster, co-founder of National Right to Life.

But Reagan, fulfilling another campaign commitment to name a woman to one of the first court vacancies of his administration, said he was satisfied O'Connor's views were in keeping with the platform.

He added effusive praise for his nominee to remarks prepared for delivery in Chicago to a fundraiser for Republican Gov. Jim Thompson Tuesday night.

Citing her "long and brilliant record" as an Arizona state legislator, Reagan called Judge O'Connor "a thoughtful, capable woman whose judicial temperament is highly appropriate for the court.

"After listening to her and examining her whole record in public life, I am fully satisfied that her appointment is consistent with the principles enunciated in our party platform this past year.

"Judge O'Connor, in my view, will bring new luster and new strength to the Supreme Court. I feel certain that her term upon the bench will be one of the proudest legacies of my presidency," Reagan said.

In its 1980 platform, the GOP promised to "work for the appointment of judges at all levels of the judiciary who respect traditional family values and the sancity of innocent life."

In announcing the appointment earlier at the White House, Reagan said he was "completely satisfied" with O'Connor's position on abortion. White House spokesman Larry Speakes said Mrs. O'Connor told Reagan during a July 1 interview that abortion was "personally abhorrent to her."

It was that Oval Office interview that clinched it for Judge O'Connor.

Boulder Valley Magazine folds after three years

'. . . a struggle to create quality': publisher

By CHIP HINDS
Colorado Daily Staff Writer

After three years of publication, the *Boulder Valley Magazine* has folded. Mike Vaughn of Cove Publications said lack of advertising support made May's issue the last.

Cove Publications, which also includes the Design Westgroup Advertising Agency, was formed last year to transform the ailing *Boulder Monthly Magazine* with a new format. The *Boulder Valley Magazine* only lasted three issues but boosted circulation from 3,800 to 7,400 copies. Unfortunately, advertising revenues did not increase proportionately. "We needed about 20 new clients," Vaughn said.

The original *Boulder Valley* began in 1978 as part of a national wave of city magazines attempting to capitalize on the reader's urban identity and provide advertisers with a way to reach a select market of educated, upper-income people in a tight geographic area. Just as the *Denver Magazine* includes its guide to the KVOD classical music station, *Boulder Monthly* listed play from KBVL.

The *Boulder Monthly* also featured regular columns on food, wine, restaurants and real estate. Longer articles covered everything from Mexican travel to cattle mutilations in Colorado.

Vaughn wanted to refocus the editorial content. "People didn't want to see an

investigative magazine," he says. "They don't want to know the latest at Rocky Flats. They want an entertaining, informative magazine that believes in a healthy generation of business in the valley."

Vaughn started the magazine with another out-of-towner, Doug Mayes, but only saw the magazine through its first two issues before returning to his consulting business in Washington, D.C. In the meantime, the publication was shepherded by a series of editors, each lasting for a

continued on page 3

Science, art go hand in hand in new Ramaley addition

Thirty artworks open with building in fall

By KAREN KOS
Colorado Daily Staff Writer

The empirical world of biological science and the subjective world of art have successfully intertwined at the new Ramaley Biology building addition, where around 30 pieces of art worth $41,000 are to be displayed when the complex opens next fall.

Two works of spiraling wood sculpture are currently visible on the north and south sides of the addition — the efforts of Denver sculptor Bob Behrens, who also created the wooden sculpture at the Denver Art Museum. The piece is called an "environmental" sculpture because it reflects the climate, orientation, local materials and the physical space constraints of its location.

During the remainder of the summer, nine other artists — four of them from Boulder — will be installing their commissioned pieces of ceramics, weaving and tapestry, photography and other artworks in the new wing, which is nearly completed.

Because of a law passed by the state legislature in 1977, public art and new buildings constructed with state funds go hand in hand. The law requires that 1 percent of the appropriation be used for the acquisition of public art for the building. that it wouldn't have had otherwise," noted Fine Arts Prof. Luis Eades, who served on a committee which selected the Ramaley art pieces.

The Colorado Council on the Arts and Humanities (CCAH, charged with administering this public art program, last year set up a five-member art selection jury for the Ramaley project — which received a total of $4.5 million for the construction of the addition in the 1979 state budget bill.

continued on page 3

Ex-prof arrested on two counts

Former sociology professor Fred Templeton was arrested Monday night by Boulder police for first-degree burglary and felony menacing, in violation of a six-month continued sentence which he received in February on a third-degree trespass charge.

Templeton, who resigned from the university last month while being investigated for "conduct below the minimum standards of professional integrity," was held in custody at the Boulder County Justice Center until Tuesday afternoon, when he was released after posting a $5,000 bond.

Daily Camera — Thursday, October 29, 1981 17

TODAY

Camera Staff Photo by Jerry Cleveland

REFLECTIONS — The scupture 'Solar Flash Flood,' by Bob Behrens of Denver glistens in the sun over Boulder Creek near the Broadway bridge. It is part of the Third Annual Sculpture in the Park Exhibition, now almost over. Behrens' entry consists of refractive tape on aluminum beams and steel cables.

At this point, the water gets very muddy.

The Eighties and Nineties

The works that Robert produced from the mid 1980s to the mid 90s, and those being presented here are only conjecture on my part as I have to work with the images that are available. Few of Robert's drawings have survived and written information is lacking.

Nevertheless, what can be discerned is that it was a period of enormous exploration and discovery for Robert. He crafted many models, wrote proposals, entered competitions, built installations, and completed some full-scale works. All along, he was assisted in these endeavors by Marga Friberg, his partner and collaborator of more than twenty-five years, and an architect in her own right. Marga was also the "soul" of the Cottage Inn and Spa, which they both designed and built in Sonoma, and where they lived during the nineties.

The next few pages may have the wrong dates and locations, but what they do demonstrate is a constant production, continual experimentation, and endless determination.

- Gary Dwyer

Light Crystal
Denver (?) 1980's ?

American Way Magazine Headquarters
Proposal - Fort Worth, Texas 1983

Winter Solstice - Denver 1980's

Uknown study model - no date or location

Uknown study model - no date or location

Illusions Space / Mass circa 1985

59

Solar Kite, Denver 1980

The City of Davis was in the process of renovating their train station and adding a bus station in the same location. Of course, they had to call the new facility *The Multi-modal Transportation Center.* And because the City has a Public Art Ordinance, competing artists were asked to submit proposals.

Davis is one of the flattest places in California because it is in a river delta has great agricultural land and has waterways whose banks are crowded with Sedges (bulrushes) which are locally known as **toolies.** My first proposal was to build giant bright colored Toolies.

My Second Proposal required me to get past identifying the place and into the idea of travel. I understood the station had to do with was arrival and departure, and that I had better understand what was inside those terms.

Even though some cultures don't do it, the act of waving seems nearly spontaneous. (The French think it rude to point and the Nepalese think it is rude to sit with your feet sticking out toward someone.) But overall, a station is a Terminus, a place where one thing ends and another one begins. It is, by extension a place of meeting and greeting, and above all, waving from a distance.

A train station is a window. A place from which we can indicate only two things: optimism or sadness.

-Editor

The winning proposal, called 'Solar Intersections,' was made by Robert Behrens and is much better than my ideas. His eloquent solution involves light and the passing of time. How perfectly appropriate for a train station.

- Gary Dwyer

Solar Intersections Davis, California circa 1985

Seen in three different lights.

Photo Credit: City of Davis / Robert Schulz, 2012

"Sculptors have traditionally used materials such as stone, wood and steel as the departure point for the development of their art. **Behrens' work uses place and sunlight.** These works are intended to give the participant viewer a new vision of place. They are sculptural spaces that exist in the special ephemeral light of each second. This momentary experience is contrasted to the weight of the unique history of each place.

This exhibition is comprised of selected site specific projects of the 1980's, in various North American locations. They are non-moving, kinetic, place-oriented artworks that are responsive to the spirit, history, atmosphere, seasonal change and other natural and man-made aspects of place. The expression of location, orientation, time/scale/space relationship and visual context give each work many layers of potential experience.

The artworks only exist in relationship to their context. Unlike transportable art which depends on the internal relationships for its meaning, these site specific artworks exist only in relationship to the physical, historical, visual and social context of each location. Each artwork is the ensemble of all these aspects which make a spirit of place."

From an Unknown exhibition.

Solar Intersections
Davis, California circa 1985

Photo © Vicky Padgett 2012 - Fairbanks

She says, "Every time I see this arch, I know I'm home."

Photo © Shelly Showwalter 2012 - Fairbanks

Publicly Funded Art Work Welcomes Interior Visitors

BY DIANA BRYSON
Staff Writer
Daily News-Miner, Fairbanks, Alaska
July 11, 1985

Welded steel, sunshine and an artist's realization work together to welcome airline travelers to the Interior.

The sculpture, recently open to public view, "Solar Borealis" peaks 50 feet above the exit of the Fairbanks International Airport, reflecting sunlight and throwing spectrum colors to viewers who approach it on a sunny day.

The $107,000 sculpture was selected above 71 other pieces submitted for the site and was paid for with funds from the state's Percent for Art Program.

San Francisco artist Robert Behrens designed the huge sculpture specifically to fit the Interior's environment. The piece can withstand harsh climates and is created to "work" with the seasons.

Special diffraction grating attached to the front of the sculpture is designed to reflect sunlight. The best time to view the sculpture in action is around 11 a.m. or noon. In the evening, when the sun is on the far side of the sculpture, the metallic trellis appears stark and silvery-white.

On a mid-winter day, when Fairbanks' color scheme is limited to black and white, the few hours of sunlight will throw some color into an otherwise dreary day.

Behrens named the sculpture Solar Borealis, which translates from Latin to "Northern Sun." He described his work as "a metaphor for the unique natural light of the north, with its long summer days and brief winter light . . . a dazzling array of spectral color against the sky, a gesture of northern lights."

Since the sculpture was completed a few weeks ago, Doyle Ruff, manager of the Fairbanks International Airport, said he has not received many comments about the airport's new art addition.

He said eventually he would like to see the piece become known as a type of trademark of the community.

Like other art pieces in public places, Solar Borealis was selected by a panel of judges who sifted through dozens of proposals submitted by artists around the country.

One of the members of the selection committee, Gary Pohl of Fairbanks, said narrowing the proposals down to a few that would survive Alaska's extreme conditions was necessary. Once the committee narrowed it to five different proposals, it was a task to select the 'piece that would be viewed and judged by thousands of people daily.
"The thing that attracted us most about this was the diffractive nature of it. It will vary with the weather and the seasons," Pohl said.

Pohl works with the architectural firm Unwin Scheben Korynta Huettl, which heads the expansion project at the airport. Finding artwork to fulfill the state's requirement that one percent of the
construction costs be spent on art isn't easy. "It's kind of difficult because of the nature of these things-such as the
sculpture in front of federal building or Nimbus in Juneau, which gets so much publicity-a lot of it negative," Pohl said.

He added that knowing how subjective artwork is, selecting an expensive and permanent piece that will be judged by countless thousands is a thoughtful process. "You try to second guess yourself and what the public would want. It took us several meetings to narrow it down to the final selection and it wasn't
an easy decision. I think that no matter what you choose, some people will resent it that money was spent on art. Art is such a selective thing anyway," he said.

Other artwork paid for by the Percent For Art Program includes a large photo-mural on stretched cloth. The photograph was taken by Ron Klein with a Circuit camera. It is 1,000 feet square and was installed about six months ago inside the airport. . .

Solar Bolearlis - Fairbanks, Alaska 1985

NORTHERN LIGHTS—This a scale model of a metal sculpture Robert Behrens will erect at the drive leading away from the Fairbanks International Airport.
(Staff photo by Eric Muehling)

Airport art underway

Construction is underway on an outdoor art project at Fairbanks International Airport which will span the exit roadway leading away from the terminal.

Crews are now preparing the foundation for the large metal sculpture, which is titled "Solar Borealis." Robert Behrens is the artist.

The sculpture was chosen by the state's Airport Art Selection Committee in 1983 from more than 200 proposals, as part of the state program under which a portion of the construction cost of new public buildings is dedicated for works of art. Its cost is $145,000.

According to airport manager Doyle Ruff, the sculpture suggests light qualities found in the Arctic atmosphere. The metal arch will be covered with diffraction grating that breaks light into its component colors, similar to the effects of a prism.

The sculpture will be visible from anywhere in front of the terminal building, and on sunny days the resulting spectral color will be visible from "quite a distance," Ruff said. On cloudy days the sculpture will appear silver.

Crews are now installing the foundation for the sculpture, and it is to be erected by the end of the month. It will be shipped to Fairbanks in sections, welded together on the ground, and then erected. Ruff said the sculptor hopes to dedicate it on the summer solstice, June 21.

Behrens has described the sculpture as "a metaphor for the special light of the north with its long summer days and brief winter light—a gesture of Northern Lights."

The indoor art project commissioned in connection with the terminal expansion is the free-hanging photo mural in the rotunda of the new terminal. It is a 365-degree photograph of Gold Dredge #3 taken with a 1925 Cirkut camera and printed on a 10-feet by 85-feet canvas panel.

Arch of colors

The "Solar Borealis" rises 50 feet above the Fairbanks International Airport exit, reflecting sunlight in a spectrum of colors to viewers who approach it on a sunny day. The $107,000 sculpture was designed by San Francisco artist Robert Behrens and paid for with funds from the state's Percent for Art Program.

Vince DeWitt/News-Miner

Photo © Vicky Padgett 2012 - Fairbanks

Model for Solar Borealis - Fairbanks, Alaska 1985

Solar Wave Garden Grove, California 1986

By Jenny Campbell
The Orange County Register

September 23 1986

A few months ago, artist Robert Behrens suffered a minor case of whiplash in an auto accident. His doctor's advice? Don't look up. Behrens has spent a lot of time lately ignoring that advice. In fact, the sculptor spends hours staring straight up to the top of the 160 foot high atrium of the ne"' Alicante Princes Hotel in Garden Grove, where his newest work is being installed.

Behrens, who is based in San Francisco, calls his 300 foot long creation "Light Wave," and it's only the latest of as many as 70 site specific pieces the former architect has created for cities. universites and other institutions. and businesses across the contient

Behrens shares his visions with Marga Friberg, who's worked as his assistant full time for about a year. Friberg also has a background in architecture; she left a job with a prestigious architectural firm in San Francisco to travel with the artist. "Marga and I together are a good combination." Behrens says. "With both our backgrounds in architecture. and my experience in art, I think we work very well together."

Three other environmental artists besides Behrens were invited to vie for the job at the hotel. which is operated by Princess Cruises and owned by dentist and real-estate mogul Dr. Robert F. Beauchamp of Newport Beach

Ross Justice. general manager of the hotel. says: "There were all kinds of weird ideas being tossed around. With this huge open space in the atrium, the possibilities were unlimited. There was a lot of talk about hanging things... like hanging papier-mache birds over the bar and all kinds of weird ideas."

Behrens, whose artistic proposal eventually beat out the competition. says, "I knew the size of the space. It's 2 million cubic feet, and with that kind of volume of space. I knew I could do something (big)." "Running a hand through his blond hair, he adds, "I mean, this place has its own atmosphere, with a domination of sky. And it became important to me to have an element that was skylike."

That sky like element is Behrens· "Light Wave." The wave, once it's in place and hanging from the 160-foot-high atrium ceiling, will be made up of 568 three-quarter-inch square aluminum rods, hung individually by thin, galvanized steel cables. Each 21 foot rod is covered by a defraction Mylar designed to catch light and reflectit in a prism of color.

And in order to understand how the sculpture Will be "skylike." you've also got to understand the Alacante Princess.

The structure, an orangish-pink behemoth at Harbor Boulevard and Chapman Avenue, can be seen from miles in any direction. The complex includes a posh 17~story hotel and an adjoining, and matching office building. The atrium, which forms a triangle between the hotel and the office building, sports a ceiling-to-floor glass facade that looks out to the northeast over the hotel parking lot, Disneyland's snow-capped Matterhom and the Santa Ana Mountains, on a clear day. Just outside the front doors is a circular fountain adorned by a nock of sculpted, 12-foot high pink flamingos.

Between the hotel and the offices, at the top of the atrium's triangle, is another series of window panels facing southwest. Through the front windows, Behrens' wave will catch the morning light, and through those back windows, the rays from the setting sun w1ll catch the wave from behind.

"It depends totally on the time of day and angle," Justice says enthusiastically "It depends purely on the lighting and the angles .... You see it differently each time you look at it; it's kinetic."

Once all 568 rods are bolted individually to a steel runner that snakes across the length of the atrium ceiling, Behrens will take to the scaffolding and fine-tune each rod. "There are these little buckles on the bolts that attach the cables to the roof." he explains. "and I'll turn those buckles to adjust the height and the lateral face so that it'll catch the light ...

Behrens, soft spoken with an easy manner and a quick sense of humor, adds that the birth of his "Light Wave" partially resulted from a visit to Alaska, where his last commission was to construct a gateway over the highway into Fairbanks.

"While I was up there. I experienced the aurora borealis, and I decided I wanted to do something like that, something that goes in and out of your experience. Something that at one point is very brilliant, at another point very subtle, something significant."

Behrens adds that the final version of his wave, which he and Friberg have been constructing since November in a spare office at the complex, was merely a refinement of what he knew all along he wanted to do.

"I did these line drawings, with quick strokes," Behrens says, demonstrating with an index finger on the wall of room 1709, as he watches a pair of iron-willed iron workers stroll nonchalantly across 160-root-hIgh beams, attaching the cables. Unperturbed by the death-defying act going on just outside the window, Behrens continues, "I just kept drawing these waves, these curves.

One year later - 1987, The notoriously underperforming Princess Alicante Hotel had been taken over by Hyatt. One of the first things Hyatt said they wanted to do was to, "brighten up the lobby." (It has sixteen stories of clear glass on the fascade.)

By 1998 the Tarsadia Group of Orange county bought the hotel and again the hotel was renovated. There is no obvious evidence of when the sculpture "Light Wave" was removed and presumably destroyed. It has simply vanished.

Photographs of the finished lobby and sculpture after final instalation are not available. - Editor.

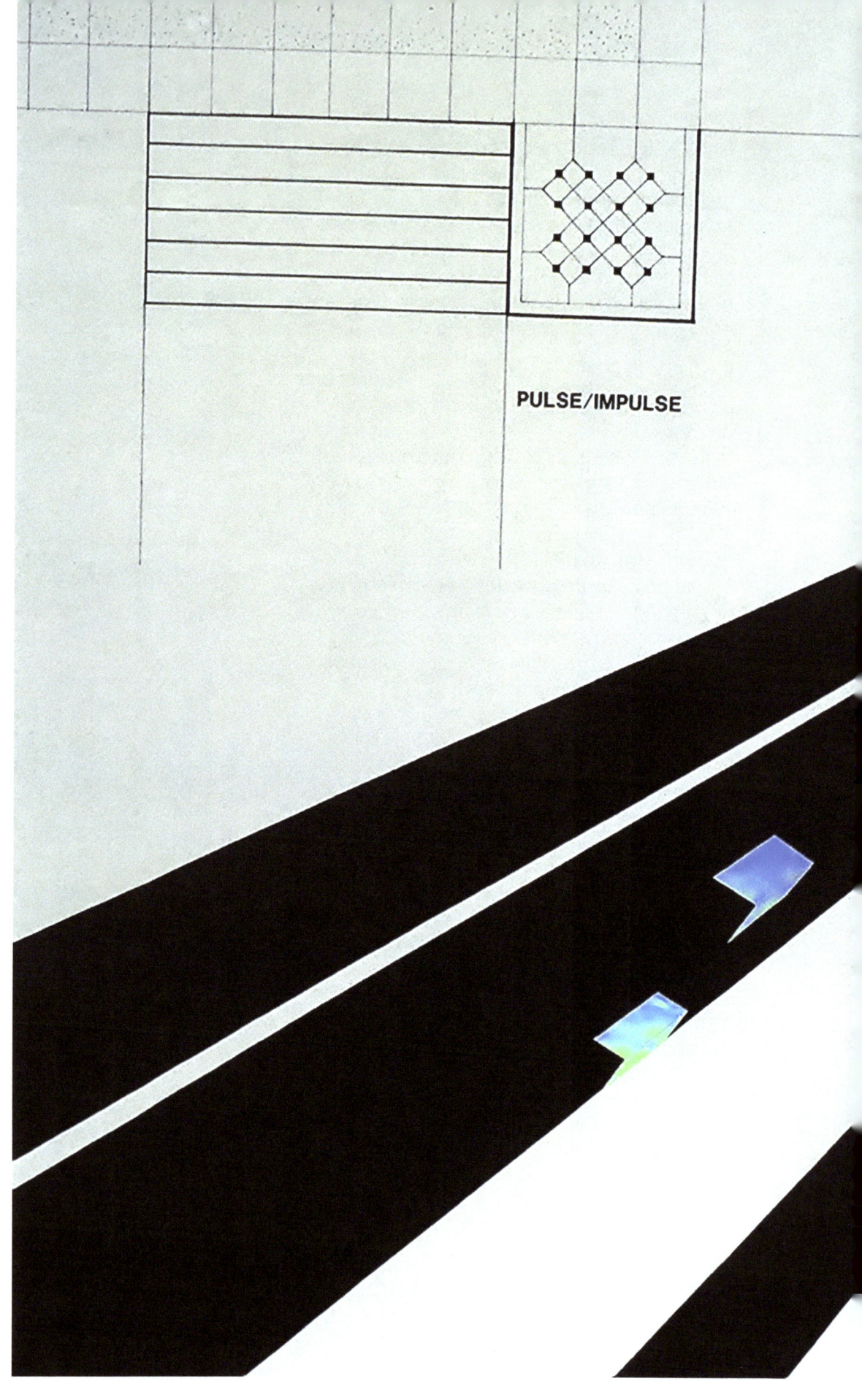

Drawing for Pulse / Impulse
University of Colorado, Colorado Springs 1985

Photo Credit: Jeffrey M. Foster 2012

Pulse / Impulse
University of Colorado, Colorado Springs 1985

Photo Credit: Jeffrey M. Foster 2012

Pulse / Impulse
University of Colorado, Colorado Springs 1985

Pulse / Impulse
University of Colorado, Colorado Springs 1985

85

Towering structure

Bob Behrens admires a collection of 16 40-foot-tall steel tubes that make up his sculpture, titled "Pulse-Impulse," after the creation's installation Monday in front of the new engineering building at the University of Colorado at Colorado Springs.

Photo Credit: Phillip Denman 2012

Pulse / Impulse
University of Colorado, Colorado Springs 1985

Sculptor of UCCS work sees things differently

By Stuart Glascock
Colorado Springs Sun

High-tech artist Robert Behrens' mind works differently than most.

It plays with bold ideas, working them over in terms of spacial patterns relative to overall environmental conditions.

Behrens

When Behrens glances west from downtown Colorado Springs, he doesn't see a famous landmark.

"It is the edge of two significant continental features," he said. "One is the plains coming in crashing against the mountains. That's a continental thing, not a local one.

"Wherever that happens, it is powerful — and Colorado Springs should respond to it."

He said extraordinary structures are built at elevations between 5,000 and 6,500 feet above sea level. Witness Mesa Verde, the Air Force Academy, the National Center for Atmospheric Research and the Johns Manfield building, he said.

"Almost everything above it and below it pales by comparison," he said.

A highly acclaimed sculptor in Colorado, Behrens' displays art in many public places in the state — at the entrance to the Denver Art Museum, at the Cherry Creek Reservoir, at the Denver Convention Center Plaza and in Vail and Boulder.

Today, the University of Colorado at Colorado Springs will join that list. A Behrens creation also will be in full public view in the courtyard of the Engineering and Applied Sciences building.

His sculpture, Pulse/Impulse, will be visible from Interstate 25.

Pulse/Impulse is composed of 16 steel columns projecting 40 feet into the sky and arranged in a grid. Starting 12 feet up, there are 6-inch squares of diffraction grating bonded to each column every 2½ feet.

When the sunlight strikes the colored squares, a field of colored light appears to move across and through the columns.

"The sculpture is going to have the appearance of being highly technical," he said. "Part of that is the way it is ordered. It's going to be very energetic, but at the same time very static, like an enormous machine."

Although the sculpture has no moving parts, the way light will move through it will give it the appearance of controlled movement. It is supposed to be suggestive of what's going on inside the building, which is highly technical, electrical, computer and physical engineering, Behrens said.

"Can you really tell it is an engineering and applied science building vs. a biology building vs. a library vs. a residence hall?" he asked.

"Part of what I'm trying to do with my artwork is to identify some of these very exclusive and perhaps unknown activities that happen within these anonymous buildings."

In the computer age, a high degree of reality is abstract, unseen. Part of Behrens objective is to translate abstract concepts into visual images that communicate chunks of abstract reality in an understandable way.

Behrens art also attempts to impart historical significance. Pulse/Impulse is no exception.

"The most dominant thing here is the mountains," he said. "Everything else is subordinate to it. Colorado mountains are so visible because of the great sunlight. When I started thinking about the history here, I thought about the great sunlight and enormous amount of visibility.

"It was very important to me to include sunlight in the work."

Explaining his lifelong pursuit, Behrens described the art of sculpturing as a process of communication.

"As I develop a piece of sculpture, it becomes more and more of a communication with other people — and less communication with myself."

A couple of days before Pulse/Impulse was set into place, Behrens said his task was to execute an idea for an image that was cultivated long ago.

Nonetheless, sheer expectation shone in his crisp, blue eyes.

"It is important for me to make what I intend to make," he said, dropping his chin slightly and looking more serious.

"What I'm trying to do now is fulfill ideas. That is what art is about."

A big idea

Sculptor's work graces UCCS

By Susan Leonard
Gazette Telegraph

At Cherry Creek State Park it was picnic shelters. At the Boulder Center for Visual Arts, it was a solar flash flood. In Colorado Springs, at the University of Colorado, it's "Pulse/Impulse," 16 black steel columns jetting 40 feet into the air at the entrance to the new Engineering and Applied Science Building.

It's public art and it's sculptor Robert Behrens' forte.

A construction crane lifted the steel beams into a 64-square-foot concrete grid Monday morning as Behrens moved around to admire his work from every imaginable angle. The artist was happy.

Some 768 squares of mylar, 48 squares per beam, reflect colored light that changes with the movement of the sun and from the viewer's perspective on the ground.

"As the sun sets, the whole thing will be a blaze of color. It probably can be seen from (Interstate) 25," Behrens said.

The sculpture is one of four pieces of art planned for the new engineering facility, James Tracey, dean of the engineering school, said. "It is absolutely fantastic," Tracey said. "Both the building and the artwork exceed our expectations."

State law requires that 1 percent of the construction budget on public buildings be set aside for works of art. In this case, about $85,000 was reserved. Pulse/pulse cost $30,000.

Behrens admits that most of his work was in the design and planning for the sculpture. "To a large degree, it is a very straightforward industrial product," he said.

Behrens and assistant Marga Friberg meticulously attached the mylar patches at 2½-foot intervals along the beams after they were professionally painted. Contractor G.E. Johnson did the heavy work — pouring concrete and erecting the beams.

Surveyors carefully lined up the beams Monday anticipating another layer of concrete that will seal the beams in place.

Robert Behrens is pleased with his "Pulse/Impulse."
Sarah Buffingwon/Gazette Telegraph

Behrens' idea was selected from those submitted by more than 200 artists to the Colorado Council for the Arts.

"The whole thrust was to make artwork that interacted in the environmental and social condition. Artwork is relative to the community. It should help identify what the facility is, help define the architecture," Behrens said.

Behrens said his sculpture defines the science facility because, like a computer, "it changes things very fast."

Connections
Oxnard, California 1988

Interest Building in Oxnard Over Landmark Tower : Officials Hope 8-Story Sculpture Near Highway Will Focus Attention on City

March 10, 1988 MEG SULLIVAN
L.A. Times Staff Writer

Most motorists think of Oxnard as the place they drive through on their way to somewhere else--such as Santa Barbara or Malibu. But not for long, if city officials get their way.

They hope that a towering piece of sculpture scheduled to be erected as early as April at Oxnard's southern border on California 1 will change all that. "Connections," as the eight-story concoction has been named by its Sonoma artist, is being touted as the burgeoning city's magnet to the tourism that keeps passing it by.

"One thing's for sure," predicts Don Rideout, management analyst for the city's Community Development Department, "people from outside the area will start to realize there's more to Oxnard than they thought."

Told Corp. of Newbury Park, the real estate developer that is paying for the sculpture under Oxnard's Art in Public Places Program, is billing "Connections" as the city's equivalent to Seattle's Space Needle--or, for that matter, the District of Columbia's Washington Monument or the Gateway Arch of St. Louis.

Officials in the city's community development department, who since 1985 have required large commercial developments to include public art, won't go that far. With two sculptures already standing, another in the works and at least nine coming down the pike, they are in no position to play favorites.

The 'Tallest Sculpture'

They do confirm, however, Told's boast that its collection of nine tightly grouped 80-foot poles, to stand at the $200-million Channel Islands Business Park, will constitute the "tallest sculpture on Highway 1 between Mexico and Canada." Apart from its annual Strawberry Festival, city officials have few tangible opportunities to pique the interest of passers-by visiting Oxnard's attractions, which include the Channel Islands Harbor. Eventually, however, they hope to lead visitors through the whole town with a map of how to find the rest of the developers' sculptures, says Rideout. In the meantime, they will count on the black steel needles to coax tourists from the highway, which is lined with taco stands, muffler shops and budget motels. Rising above the rapidly developing Oxnard Plain, the work is expected to be visible for up to four miles, vying for attention with Oxnard's two high-rise office buildings.

"This is definitely going to be a vertical landmark," says Rideout.

The 48-year-old artist, Robert Behrens, says his similarly shimmering gateway to Fairbanks, Alaska, is the largest piece of modern sculpture in that state. But mere attention was not what the developer was after, said V. Patrick Hall, president of Told. Rather, the firm's officials were wowed by Behrens' high-tech materials.

Company officials thought Behrens could best evoke the capabilities of its "smart park" site, which will be outfitted with fiber-optic networks to accommodate the latest in computer and data transmission equipment.

In fiber optics, Behrens said, "there is a pulse of information sent through lines of fiber as pieces of light and recombined into information. It's the same thing with "Connections." There are discrete pieces of light that make patterns that change as people approach the site." That quality stems from the artist's liberal use of Mylar, a refracting surface that makes his works glow with an eerie incandescence that changes color as the viewers approach and recede.

The plastic material gives the poles the dynamic quality "of moving art such as a water fountain without the problems or expense," Hall said.

Planning officials, meanwhile, gave Behrens a green light for another reason. They say his piece embodies the informal guidelines for its Art in Public Places Program, which calls for "something that complements the building but suggests some other values," Rideout said. They think its linear characteristics mimic those of the 135 yet-to-be-constructed buildings at the business park that will play home to tenants as diverse as the County of Ventura and Mercedes-Benz of America. At the same time, they say, the sculpture raises viewers' sights far, far above the park, a former celery field. "Its going to make people look skyward," says Rideout. "And by emphasizing the colors and the sun, it hopefully will give people an appreciation of the outdoors, sunlight, color patterns—something other than the working world."

At the very least, the sculpture, which will be imitated in two smaller pieces elsewhere in the park, is supposed to provide a spoonful of sugar for the medicine of economic development, Rideout says. He predicts the sculpture will "give something back to the people of Oxnard. When there is development in a city . . . certain intangibles are lost."

Clusters of Public Art Might Again Stand Out ON THE ROAD

July 28, 1994 LEONARD REED

Leonard Reed is a L. A. Times staff writer

OXNARD — The southward ride from Oxnard to the Pacific Coast Highway at Point Mugu is one of urban deliverance: from clanking muffler shops, used auto yards and seedy strip joints to vast verdant vegetable fields to muscular mountains that vault from the ocean.

The liberating gray-to-blue progression is broken only by the poles. The poles: Nine of them, clustered together, each a foot wide and deep but a towering 80 feet tall. You've seen them, possibly.

They stand at the junction of Rose Avenue at Oxnard Boulevard, on the northwest corner just down a piece from Marie Callender's. They're painted black. Each has a series of silver bands, spaced tightly at the top and loosely in the middle and then far apart at the bottom.

For the literal-minded among us, the poles might appear as radar or some stealth navigation device--Point Mugu Naval Air Station is nearby, after all. For others whose viewpoint slides more easily into the surreal, the poles might stand as a mutant shock of horsetail from some space giant's garden. However these steel columns appear, though, they do not look like what they are: art.

But they started out as art, and more plainly so.

In 1988 the Told Corp., a builder of industrial parks, agreed to the city of Oxnard's request that its proposed development include public art--that is, art that Told would pay for and place on its private property, but that would be designed on such a monumental scale as to transcend property lines and become art in the public domain. The poles do that, at least the get-noticed part.

Told hired Sonoma artist Robert Behrens to do the job. Behrens is a national player in the public art world. Massive sculptures by Behrens connect the New Orleans Super Dome to the Mississippi River, form a civic gateway across the main highway leading into Fairbanks, Alaska, and lend energy and changing light to the railroad station in Davis. Indeed, Behrens' Davis piece is so prominent and familiar there that it must now be taken into account as a governing design consideration in development that goes up around the railroad station.

Behrens was struck by Told's decision to develop an industrial campus without traditional copper phone wiring and instead install fiber optics--a telecommunications medium of the future. He also was struck by Oxnard's desire to transcend the look of rusting South Oxnard Boulevard by giving northward travelers a gateway into a high-tech, forward-looking city. "It needed to be a powerful enough statement amid all the mundane, amid the muffler shops, to say something about the future," says Behrens.

So Behrens conceived of the poles. The towering cluster is joined by three other pole groupings, though you might not have noticed them: 11 in one long line, and nine more in a cluster, at the junction of Statham and Oxnard boulevards, at the west end of the property, and a cluster of nine, perhaps 30 feet tall, at the corner of Rose and Wooley avenues, at the far northeast end of the property.

The silver bands on the poles are a special formulation of Mylar, which refracts daylight every which way. Behrens positioned the Mylar on the poles so that at sunrise or sunset, especially, passersby would suddenly see changing bright colors, as if green-blue-golden rainbows within each group magically connected all the poles. Placement of the poles became critical: They needed enough light and enough space around them to be seen.

Behrens named his serial installation "Connections," and "Connections" would, fired up by Nature, become a bright post-Industrial metaphor "linking light, time, space and people," to quote a mud-caked plaque at the base of the poles at Wooley and Rose.

For a while it worked. The Mylar seemed electrified. The poles stood out on their own.

But Told's once-singular industrial park got sold off in pieces, and its open spaces filled up. All manner of buildings went up near and around the poles, occluding some from view and stuffing visual clutter behind others. Marie Callender's was boldest of all. The entire front of its building at Statham and South Oxnard Boulevard noses within five feet of the 11-pole array--a true astonishment of modern-day non-planning. Then, by 1992, the Mylar gave out. Behrens had underestimated the rapacity of ocean air: once-refractive material turned dull, lightless, hopeless: a conductor of nothing.

"Connections" started coming apart, started its descent into disconnection. It became poles, not art. A $250,000 set of very odd poles.

"I don't think it carries the original desires of the artist," says a diplomatic Andrew Voth, director of the Carnegie Museum and member of the city's Art in Public Places Committee. "It's totally lost. I don't blame the artist. It just did not quite come off." We'll see. "Connections" now fights for an improbable comeback.

Mylar replacement is under way, and the poles near Callender's are firing off colors that change with the slightest movement by the viewer--that is, for the viewer who manages to block out the view of the restaurant. Other pole clusters, such as the 80-foot mega-tower at Rose and South Oxnard Boulevard, await new Mylar--though that cluster at times gets lost in a row of telephone poles behind it.

As for Behrens, Oxnard provides a sobering civic jolt. "We had no idea that Marie Callender's or any other buildings would be up that close," he says. "Now the piece is distracted from by simple disregard. No one ever called me--not once--to discuss what appropriate designs on surrounding property would be. Public art, you know, is no different than anything else: It is modified by what is placed next to it."

That's a statement that lends "Connections," at least as far as land-use planning goes, a whole new meaning.

THE STANFORD DAILY

An Independent Newspaper

VOLUME 190, NUMBER 43 — 94TH YEAR — WEDNESDAY, NOVEMBER 26, 1986

Student forum looks at grove plan

By CHRIS MYERS
Editorial staff

The preliminary design for Centennial Grove was received enthusiastically at a student forum on University building and planning held last night at Tresidder Memorial Union.

The forum, organized by student representatives from the University Committee on Land and Building Development (UCLBD), was designed to educate students about the process of University planning and development and to elicit student response to the process, using the Centennial Grove project as a focus and test case.

Centennial Grove is a planned landscaping and sculpture project intended to honor donors to Stanford during its first 100 years and to provide a place to recognize future benefactors of the University.

The grove will be located at the northwest (mathematics) corner of the Quad, running parallel to Serra Street on one side and the Varian Physics Building parking lot on the other. The new grove is designed to be similar to Dohrman Grove, the grove of redwood trees situated between the Graduate School of Business and the University Art Gallery near the Quad's northeast (history) corner.

According to Centennial Grove project manager John Kennedy of the University Facilities Project Management, the dual goals in the design of the grove were "to honor donors and to create an area that invites people to use it."

University planners hope the grove will be ready for May 14, 1987, ceremonies commemorating the 100-year anniversary of the laying of the University's cornerstone.

At last night's forum, Kennedy presented a scale model and schematic drawings of the proposed design of the grove.

Students and community members attending the forum were universally pleased with the design.

"I really like it," said senior Heather Stone, one of the forum's organizers and a student representative on the UCLBD. "I think it's really something that can be majestic."

"I think it's excellent," said Heidi Hansen, a 1980 Stanford graduate and now a Palo Alto architect. "It's nice and clear conceptually.... It will function very nicely."

Several students at the forum, while expressing approval of the design, raised questions about student involvement in the University's planning process.

The design "is aesthetically great, and it meets criteria set for it," said Tom Strand, a graduate student in resources planning. "But I'm really concerned about who came up with the idea of a place to honor donors... and at what point students can plug into that (decision-making) process.

"We don't want to throw a bug into the works, but there is a point where student input becomes crucial," he said.

Last night's forum, the first of its kind, was a start toward increased student involvement in the University planning process, according to UCLBD student representative Jane Woodward, an MBA student who organized the forum along with Stone.

"We're just trying to open up the process," Woodward said. "If we can get a core of people who are interested, I think that's a good thing.... The nature of the decisions (made by the UCLBD) has to do with aesthetics; if you have two students representing 13,000, it's bound to be biased."

"I think this forum is a really good way for us (students) to get input in the process," said junior Craig Young.

Kai Keasey/Daily
A scale model of the proposed design for Centennial Grove was presented in last night's student forum.

97

Centennial Grove competition, Stanford University, 1986

Robert Behrens

Concept

Centennial Grove is a dynamic monument celebrating 100 years of Stanford's rich history and reaching 100 years into its future.

Site

The Grove is a 1.5 acre, slightly sloping site of many mature 'trees adjacent to the historic heart of the campus, the Main Quad. The site is also close to other significant campus landscaped space and artworks. The campus landscape is a juxtaposition of the formal, manicured treatment of outdoor space, i.e. the Oval, versus the informal, rural and even unruly character, the Farm.

The entire Centennial Grove site is considered a microcosm of the University and is the artwork. It is conceived as on ongoing project taking 100 years to complete. The site is bounded by a granite walk and a low level wall which merges with the walk and rises to 18" above grade at the lowest point of the site. This wall is the symbolic boundary of the University. Within the walls is an arid landscape with existing mature oaks and several large cedars and pines. All of the trees on the site are preserved. The site has large areas of open sun and dense shade.

Viewpoint

About 300' from the eastern edge is the most powerful single point on the site. This is a place of recollection and presence. Located in the open sun, an observer is given a framed view looking east to the main historic quad and Hoover Tower beyond (the past). Also, from this point, is a clear view to the west (the future) and to the yet unbuilt fountain which is the focus of the new 41 acre Near West Campus. To celebrate this particular place is to link the past accomplishments with future aspirations.

The Hyperquad / The Colonnade

The hyperquad is located near this powerful intersection. The hyperquad is composed of two quadrangles juxtaposed to each other. One, "the vessel", is aligned with the current campus grid. The other, "the colonnade" or physical university, is aligned to the new fountain focus of the new Near West Campus and juxtaposed to the vessel. Conceptually, the hyperquad is cut from one solid sandstone slab measuring 45'x53'x22". A grid of 100 22" cubes are removed and moved in formation to become the bases for 100 square bronze tubes with a diffraction surface. The diffraction will divide sunlight into spectral color, changing colors on a momentary basis. Each disk will represent a one million dollar contribution to the University. Each disk will be inscribed with the donors name and the date of the contribution, beginning with Leland Stanford in 1887 and ending with the last contribution in the year 2087. The entire colonnade will change form over the next 100 years as stone disks are added. In 100 years, there will be a total of 1000 disks.

The Hyperquad / The Vessel

The vessel is the container of ideas and is composed of the remaining stone
blocks. These blocks are laid out in a double row suggestive of the arcade
foundation surrounding the main quad. Each stone block is engraved with the
1ntellectual accomplishments of members of the Stanford community and the names
of those who made them and when they were made.

The vessel is an outdoor room of contemplation and solitude. Partially
shaded by oaks and open to the sky, the floor of the room is a smooth green lawn.
The stoneblocks can be used as seats and accommodate a class.
The hyperquad can be the setting for baccalaureates and other outdoor events.

The Intersection

At the point where the vessel and the colonnade intersect, the observer can
view both the Hoover Tower to the east and the new Near West Campus fountain to t~
west. The vessel is contemplative and internal and anchored to the earth.
The colonnade grid is dynamic and active and reaches both to the sky and the
future.

The entire ensemble is an artwork of different time frames. It is a dynamic
monument that changes in color and form over a matter of seconds and a century.
Together, Centennial Grove is an artwork that celebrates people, place, and
ideas in a time continuum.

If I remember right, this proposal should have been the winning entry, but,
there were some last minute shenanigans that went on between the clients, jurors and other finalist teams.
I know it was a heart-breaker for Marga and Robert.
There is no evidence on the web of any project ever having been built.

- Gary Dwyer

Time/Span
Competition entry for Mattapan Square - Boston Massachusetts
1992

Robert Behrens

"We shall not cease from exploration.
And the end of all exploration will be to arrive where we started
and know the place for the first time."

T.S. Eliot

Time/Span
Concept:

Time/Span is an artwork conceived and developed as a site specific response to the scale, form, light, color, movement, people and cultural history of Mattapan Square. The artwork is a reflection of my response to this cityscape, both seen and unseen. It is an artwork that bridges the past with the present, combining immediate time and movement with historical time.

Time/Span, "a cultural bridge", will dramatically transform space. Mattapan Square will change from "a way", a six lane highway street, to a clearly defined "place". Time/Span will create gateways at each end of the Square, one at River Street and one at Babson Street. The gateways will define Mattapan Square linking both sides of the street. With the buildings on the west side of the street forming one wall, building on the east side forming another; the gateways will create an implied "room" with entries at each end. The goal will be to create a more pedestrian friendly area where autos move at a slower pace and where pedestrian crossing the street can be accommodated

Time/Span is a gateway to Boston. Time/Span will give Mattapan a distinct image. Time/Span forms a plane of colored light that creates entry. All motorists on Blue Hill Parkway will drive through the artwork to enter Boston and Mattapan Square and then again as they leave the Square's shopping district. To the motorists, it is a driving through experience, to the pedestrian, it is a visual experience of defining a space. When entered from the south, Time/Span will frame St. Angela's Church and will take attention away from the view to the billboards mounted on buildings. The sculpture will be experienced by thousands of people each day in automobiles and hundreds of people on foot Both will have unencumbered visual access to the artwork affecting a maximum number of people. By raising the artwork image 20 feet above the roadway, it is visible without visual interference of building, signs, automobiles, busses and other competing distractions that occur at the street level.

Time/Span is a celebration of the people of a special place. High above the moving traffic, the arch, made up of individual steel rods, will shimmer in a rainbow of colors symbolizing the harmonious multicultural heritage of Mattapan. Each individual rod works like individuals in the community. Varied individuals, working together, create harmony; working together, the individual rods create a rainbow of colored light and harmony.
An open frame will grow out of the masonry base at both the north and the south gates. With the help of community members in the selection, the frames will hold transparent images of people, who have lived in, and contributed to, Boston and Mattapan. The south gate will celebrate people from Boston and Mattapan throughout history. The north gate will celebrate the future and the children and youth from Mattapan.

The artwork is composed of a brick base that holds steel tubing welded to form square frames. At the north gate, these stand as columns on either side of the roadway. On the south, the steel frames rise and then bridge over the roadway. These frames will hold polycarbonate panels that have been silkscreened with photographic images. Sunlight shining through the transparent images in the frames, under certain lighting conditions, will cast images on the sidewalk and roadway, affording an interesting pattern of light and dark on the plain concrete surface.

At the south gate, the community members of Boston and Mattapan are celebrated in images of people who have lived in this place and community of Mattapan and who have contributed to it. The photos will start with the Indians in the lower panels on each side. Each panel will then depict a different image of people, through colonizations and the revolution to the immigration of the Irish, the Jewish, and Afro-American at the center. Care should be taken to celebrate the cultures of Mattapan throughout the history of the area On the east island where pedestrians can come close to the base, a panel will be located to describe the images in each frame. The north gate tower would be devoted to images of youth of today in the community. The incomplete bridge suggests possibilities and challenges of the future that they face.

Light/Rain
Arvada Colorado (late 1980's ?)
Robert Behrens

Narrative Concept

Light/Rain on Chief Rain-in-the-Face, is an Artwork conceived and developed as a site specific response to the scale, form, light, color, movement, landscape, people and cultural history of Arvada. The artwork is a reflection of my response to this site, both seen and unseen. It is an artwork that is a transition from past, present and future combining immediate time and movement with historical time. The artwork is also a transition from outside to inside, from soft to hard. ·

Light/Rain on Chief Rain-in-the-Face will transform the plaza space to a place, at once making historical reference to the Native American myths, to ranching and the mini-ranches of the new Arvada. The planes of colored light will play constantly changing with the mood of the day, bringing sky to earth. The planes are a response to the fragmented view of the mountains from the plaza. The skyline of the artwork is the skyline of Chief Rain-in-the-Face Mountain and celebrates the myth of a man becoming a mountain. The Artwork is symbolic of old and new joined together to experience this place in a new way.

The artwork for many will only be seen passing in an automobile on their way to some other place, giving a flash of color and light. For others, it will break the bright sun of a summers day, with the trumpet vine trailing down from overhead, giving welcome shade. The view from above will be the skyline of distant mountains echoed in the Artwork and the colored transparent planes will reveal the blooms of the trumpet vine. The planes of colored light will constantly change as the sun moves and as the observer moves creating a 3 dimensions light painting. Light /Rain can be many different experiences to different people.

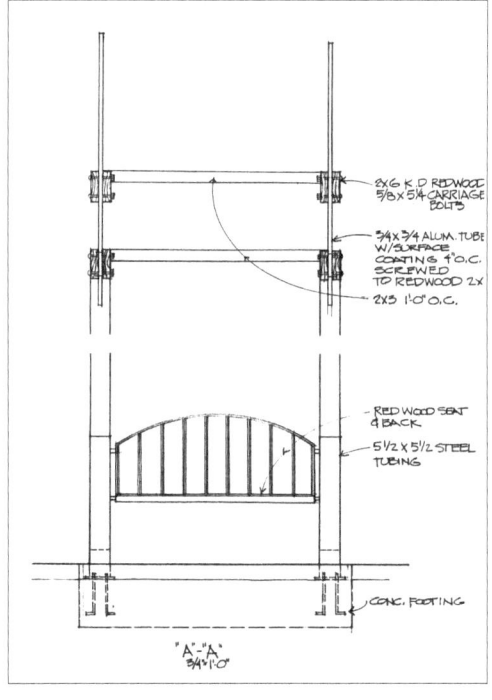
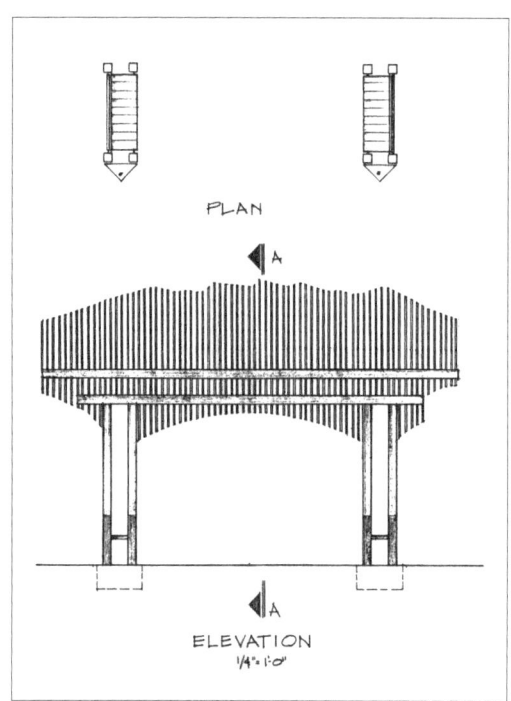

Cambridge Datum

(Competition Entry - late 1980's ?)
Robert Behrens

A Narrative Description

Siting, Materials, Color, Dimensions

Cambridge Datum is a series of 6 square fields located along Massachusetts Avenue. Each of the six fields is intended to give a precise orientation to the surrounding buildings and streetscape to the cardinal points, North, South, East and West. Each location will be given a new sense of spatial relationships between itself and the world context of longitude and latitude.

Each field is composed of a 3 dimensional orthogonal grid, 10' on center, creating a uniform field of one foot squares. The fields vary~ from 100' square to 81' square. The uniformity of the fields are only maintained on the ground plane, as a two dimensional pattern. These fields of uniformity and constant orientation magnify and celebrate the unique configuration of the surrounding streetscape and buildings by contrasting each place to a similar field. The fields are occasionally interrupted by buildings, but the overall configuration is maintained intact. The field will connect important civic buildings and spaces to the streetscape and to each other. As illustrated in Board #3 and the model, the field will also place emphasis on the pedestrian character of Mass. Ave., reducing the role of the automobile and providing greater sense of respect for people on foot. As each field encounters the pedestrian zones of the sidewalks and traffic islands, 20 foot granite columns emerge from the one foot squares. At 10' up the column, 1'square blocks of granite are covered with diffraction grating. The column is capped with a cube of granite covered with a diffraction material .On the walkways, between the columns, a 1' wide granite pavers will link to the columns and the field in the roadway.

The granite pavers and the columns will be a diary of the particular neighborhood in which each field is located. The diary will include the events and people which have shaped the land and what has been placed on the land. The granite pavers will have inscriptions and images of the events which have had an affect on the physical changes on this place. The granite monuments will have the inscriptions of the acknowledgements of the people who have lived in this neighborhood and have either affected the neighborhood or the world. The inscriptions ~ include poetry, images and narratives. The acknowledgements will beginat the settlement of Cambridge and will continue to the present and be added to each year until the year 2000. Each inscription can be determined by community selection and executed by local artists.

The columns are a record of change in decades and centuries. The light field which will move through the columns instantaneously because of the diffraction grating will mark immediate time.The changes of spectral color produced by the interactive experience between the viewer and the sun will be juxtaposed to the solidity of the granite column.

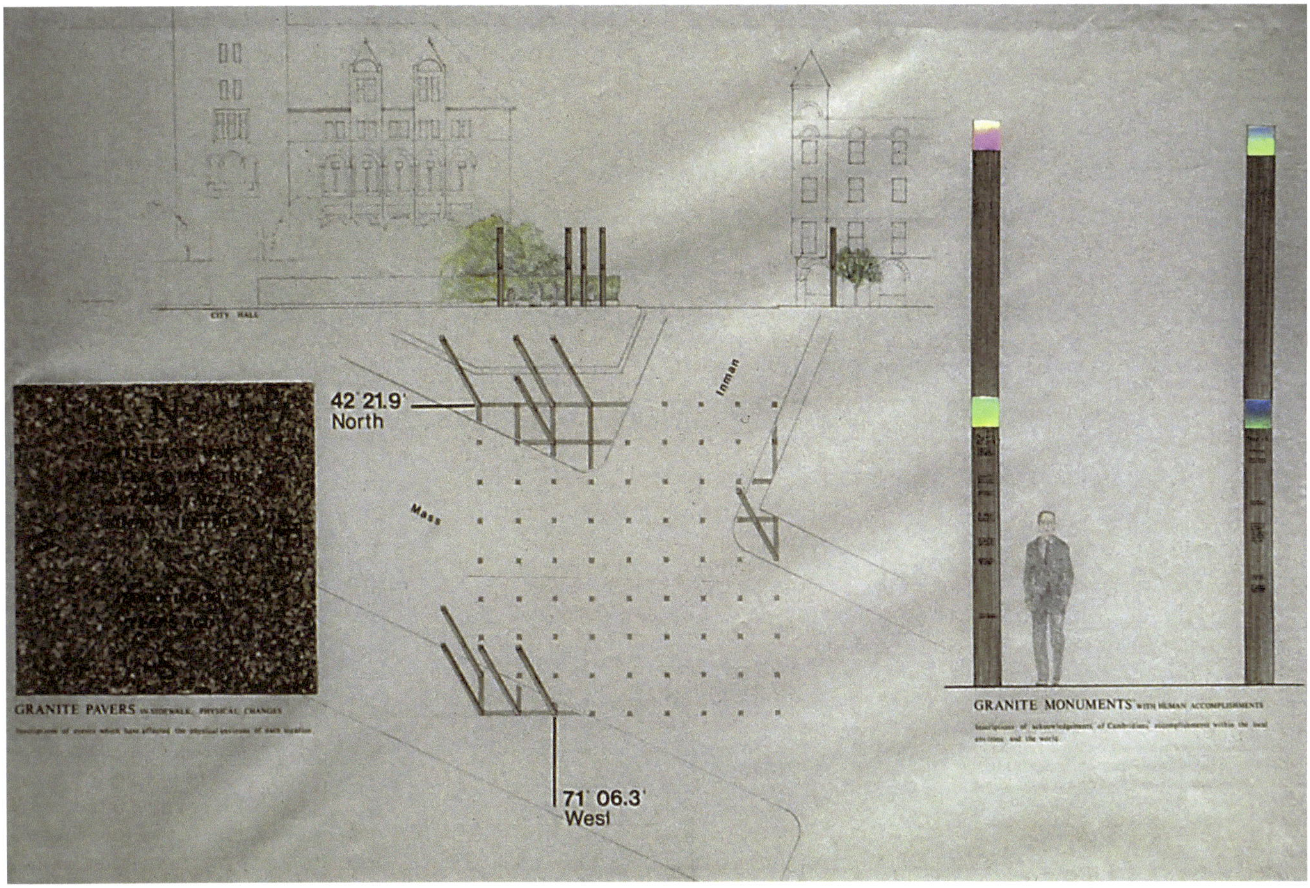

42° 21.9' North

71° 06.3' West

GRANITE PAVERS AS SIDEWALK, PHYSICAL CHANGES

GRANITE MONUMENTS WITH HUMAN ACCOMPLISHMENTS

105

LOOKING EAST

Neptune's Gate at Lafayette Place,
New Orleans, Louisiana circa 1992

"The artwork is many layered, it creates a place for people, a sense of celebration, a dynamic active environment that changes from hour to hour, day to day and season to season. It suggests history without parroting it. It is an entry gate and a focal point that reaches for the sky." - *Robert Behrens*

Vetrans Memorial Park Sonoma, California   1997-2005

Vetrans Memorial Park Sonoma, California   1997-2005

Vetrans Memorial Park Sonoma, California - Dedication Cerimonies 2005

"**Robert Behrens didn't confine art to a single sculpture or project.** He envisioned his entire city as a work of art. A public artist and designer of urban spaces and landscapes, he once brazenly applied for a National Endowment for the Arts grant to design the entire city of Sonoma as a work of urban art.

Although he was turned down, Behrens was never deterred by his failures. During his more than 20 years in the city of Sonoma, he vociferously spoke out for the aesthetic details -- large and small -- that make a street, a sidewalk, a new building, a development or a monument, something pleasing to experience and behold. An indefatigable advocate whose impassioned voice was repeatedly heard at City Hall, Behrens died Saturday (February 16, 2008) at home after a six month battle with cancer. He was 68.

"He helped change forever the way we see our own city," said former Councilman Larry Barnett. "Robert had a real appreciation for the pricelessness of the physical spaces and structures that make up a community. He kept pointing people in the direction of not making those decisions casually, and understanding that once something was built, it would be there for 50 or 100 years."

Behrens' most visible legacy is the design of the Sonoma Veterans Memorial Park in Mountain Cemetery, including a monumental five-pointed star on which are etched the names of Sonoma Valley veterans who have died. But he also is credited with the idea of making Broadway a grand passageway into the city. Many of his big ideas for creative urban design were ahead of their time, but his idea of planting oaks along the city's major gateway came to pass.

The Teaneck, N.J., native's training in the fine arts, architecture and design gave him a uniquely broad view. He attended the Pratt Institute School of Architecture in New York, got a bachelor's degree in industrial design and sculpture from the Kansas City Art Institute, studied landscape architecture at the University of Wisconsin's Graduate School of Environmental Design and earned a master's degree in sculpture from the University of Denver.

"Everything was about beauty. The simplest thing, such as putting food on the plate, looked like art," recalled his wife, Faye Behrens, his partner in the Cottage Inn and Spa several blocks from the Sonoma Mission. "To Robert, everything was art. He could do it all, and life was a celebration."

He was a leader in the effort to create an urban growth boundary, coming up with a plan that didn't sacrifice affordable housing, Barnett said. But he also was instrumental in getting the city to enact specific design guidelines for the town and was involved in the city's 1995 General Plan, which won an award from the state.

He served on the Planning Commission and lost a run for the City Council in 2002. But most of his work was as a citizen activist. With his signature dark turtleneck and soft-spoken voice, he managed to press hard while always coming across as an unfailing gentleman. "He accomplished more as an ordinary individual than most people who have sat on commissions and councils for many years," Barnett said. Behrens was an accomplished public artist whose career spanned 34 years and included projects all over the country, including the Solar Borealis Gateway at the Fairbanks International Airport in Alaska, Neptune's Gate at the entry to Lafayette Place in New Orleans and his favorite, a series of whimsical shade shelters shaped like whales tales and birds at the Cherry Creek State Recreation Area in Denver. He had a surprising footnote deep in his past. As a dapper young man he served a regular stint on TV's "The Mickey Mouse Club," doing feature spots as the club reporter."

- Meg McConahey, The Press Democrat
  Sonoma California

The Cottage Inn and Spa, Sonoma California

Designed and built by Marga Friberg and Robert Behrens. A project spanning from the late 1980's to 2000

Robert Behrens
2182 Green Street
San Francisco, California 94123
415•922•8365

12 years of independent experience in highly creative site specific sculpture, architecture, and site design, with full design responsiblities from concept to completion. Recognized leader in innovative public art in the Rocky Mountain West, receiving awards for excellence from the A.I.A. and a grant from the N.E.A. Work has been published in Progressive Architecture, Architectural Record, "Ideas, Ingenious, Bold, Playful" and recently published in *Guide to U.S. Architecture 1940-1980*, one of ten projects representing forty years of Colorado history. Juror for the A.I.A and A.S.L.A. Design Awards Program, Colorado Council on the Arts and Humanities Per Cent for Art Program. Strongly involved with the development of quality urban spaces utilizing imaginative solutions. Extensive successful collaborations with architects and landscape architects.

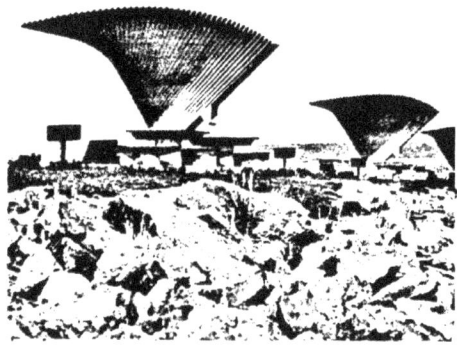

Prior Experience
University of Colorado, Graduate School of Architecture; leading design studio, Thesis Advisor, Visiting Lecturer

G. Cabell Childress, F.A.I.A., Denver, Colorado; Project Architect, Designer

University of Denver; Design Instructor

University of Colorado, School of Architecture; Visiting Critic

Wright-Ingraham Institute, Elizabeth, Colorado; Visiting Artist

Loretto Heights College, Denver, Colorado; Visiting Artist

Metropolitan State College, Denver, Colorado; Visiting Artist

Colorado College, Colorado Springs, Colorado; Visiting Artist

California State Polytechnic University, San Luis Obispo, California; Visiting Critic

References available

Education
University of Denver, Graduate School of Art, M.A. Sculpture 1972, Allied Arts Grant

University of Wisconsin, Graduate School of Environmental Design, Landscape Architecture 1966, Graduate Fellowship

Kansas City Art Institute, B.F.A. Industrial Design, Sculpture 1965, I.D.S.A. Award of Achievement, Alcoa Student Merit Award

Pratt Institute, School of Architecture 1964

Travel
49 states, Canada, Mexico, Bahamas, Italy, Greece, Switzerland, France, The Netherlands, Denmark, Norway, Sweden, England, Germany

Project Experience
selected list

Fairbanks International Airport, City Gateway, Solar Borealis, Fairbanks, Alaska

Cherry Creek State Recreation Area, Picnic Shelters, Denver, Colorado

Cherry Creek State Recreation Area, Beach Facilities, Project Architect, Denver, Colorado; G. Cabell Childress Architects

Denver Convention Center Plaza, Earth Crystal, Denver, Colorado; Muchow, Reams, Larsen Architects

Denver Art Museum, permanent Entrance Sculpture, Denver, Colorado; Gio Ponti, James Sudler Architects

Beaver Creek Town Center Plaza, Vail, Colorado; Arley Rhinehart Architect

Meadow Creek Mall, concept of water feature; Royston, Hannamoto, Beck and Abbey Landscape Architects

University of Colorado, Ramaley Hall Entry Sculpture, Boulder, Colorado; Caudill Architects

University of Denver, main Quadrangle Sculpture, Denver, Colorado

Steel Street Fountain, Urban Fountain, Denver, Colorado; Colaboration with G. Dwyer

Micro-Geophysics Corporation, site design, Denver, Colorado

Denver Technological Center, D.T.C. 40 site and plaza, Denver, Colorado; Barker, Rinker, Seacat Architects

Ambleside Park, Symbolic Gateway to Vancouver, West Vancouver, Canada

Thornton City Center, Atrium Sculpture, Lakewood, Colorado; Erickson Associates, Landscape Architects

Greenwood Recreation Center, Entrance Sculpture, Lakewood, Colorado; Erickson Associates, Landscape Architects

Boulder Center for the Visual Arts, Solar Flash Flood, Boulder, Colorado

Acknowledgements
Alaska State Council on the Arts, Fairbanks International Airport, National Competition, First Place, 1983

Intercontinental Alliance, Colorado Representative Artist to Munich, 1982

American Academy in Rome Finalist, 1981

Colorado Council on the Arts and Humanities, Per Cent for Art, University of Colorado Regional Competition, First Place, 1981

Pan American Sculpture Symposium, International Competition Winner, 1977

National Endowment for the Arts, Art in Public Places Grant, Earth Crystal, 1975

Colorado Design Assembly, Cherry Creek Shelters cited as Exemplary Design Solutions, 1975

American Institute of Architects Western Regional Citation Award, Cherry Creek Picnic Shelters, 1973

American Institute of Architects, Honor Awards Program, North Dakota, Juror, 1980

American Society of Landscape Architects, Honor Awards Program, Colorado, Juror 1978

Colorado Council on the Arts and Humanities, Art in Public Places, Juror

Denver Art Museum, "Urban Art" with I.M. Pei, Ira Licht, George Sugarman, Panelist

Colorado Council on the Arts and Humanities, "Public Art", "Artist and Potential", Lecturer

Colorado Society of Architects, "Public Art?", Lecturer, Panelist

Publications
selected list

Art in Public Places, Beardsley, Partners for Livable Places, 1981

Guide to U.S. Architecture: 1940-1980, Ester McCoy, Barbara Goldstein, Art and Architecture Press, 1982

Architectural Crafts, a Handbook and a Catalog, Bridget Beattie McCarthy, Madronna Publishers, 1982

Sculptor International, "Commissions, Sculpture as Regional Symbol", July 1984

Art Space, "Bob Behrens at Inkfish, Denver", April 1981

Progressive Architecture, "Sculpture Reflects the City", November, 1977

L'industria Italiana del Cemento, "Fuori Testo", October 1976

Architectural Record, "Design for Recreation", November 1975

Architectural Record, "Ideas, Ingenious, Bold, Playful", August 1975

Robert Karl Behrens
1939-2008

Representative Clients

State and Federal Agencies

State of Colorado, Department of Parks and Recreation
State of Washington, Art in Public Places Program
State of Colorado, Colorado Council of the Arts and Humanities
United States, National Endowment for the Arts

City Agencies

City of Denver, Denver Art Museum
City of Denver, Colorado
City of Boulder, Colorado
City of Littleton, Colorado
City of Seattle, Washington
City of West Vancouver, British Columbia, Canada
City of Sterling, Colorado
City of Vail, Colorado
City of Lakewood, Colorado

Universities, Colleges, Schools

University of Colorado, Boulder
University of Denver
University of Southern Colorado
Wright Ingraham Institute, Colorado Springs, Colorado
Arapahoe Community College
Denver School Board

Corporations, Developers

Micro Geophysics Corporation
Victoria Corporation
Chevron Distributing Company
Vail Associates
Sherman Agency
Photosynthesis
Denver Technological Center
Gary Operating Company
Urban Investment Company
Barkers Bank in Middleton, Ohio
Ed Will Development Corporation
Michael of the Carlyle

Architects, Landscape Architects

Barker, Rinker, Seacat
G. Cabell Childress Architects
Arley Rhinehart and Associates
Royston, Hannamoto and Beck and Abbey, Lanscape Architects
Lifescape Inc. Landscape Architects
Erickson Landscape Architects
Carl Worthington Associates
Abo-Gude Architects
Peter Orleans, Architects

Education

1982   Independent study in Scandanavia, Denmark, Sweden, Norway, and Germany

1978   Independent study in Italy and Greece

1972   Masters of Arts, Sculpture, University of Denver, Denver, Colorado

1971   Independent study in Mexico

1967   Graduate Fellowship, University of Wisconsin, Madison, Wisconsin

1966   Alcoa Student Merit Award

1966   Industrial Designer Society's of America Award of Achievement

1966   Graduate study, Environmental Design, University of Wisconsin, Madison, Wisconsin

1966   Bachelor of Fine Arts, Industrial Design, and Sculpture, Kansas City Art Institute, Kansas City, Missouri

1964   Architectural Studies, Pratt Institute, Brooklyn, New York

1961   Art studies, Kansas City Art Institute, Kansas City, Missouri

1957   Graduated Pascack Valley High School, Hillsdale, New Jersey

Exhibitions

1982   Inkfish Gallery, Denver, Colorado

1982   *Wright Ingraham Institute, Running Creek Field Station, Elbert, Colorado, "Datum"

1982   Boulder Visual Arts Center, Sculpture in the Park, "Solar Flash Flood"

1981   Inkfish Gallery, Denver, Colorado, One Man Show, "Wood Revolutions of Scale"

1981   *University of Colorado, Boulder, Colorado, Environmental Sculpture, "Line Fragments"

1980   Arvada Center for the Arts, Arvada, Colorado, "Colorado Percent for Art Program"

1979   Boulder Visual Arts Center, Sculpture in the Park, "Contour Drawings"

1979   Gallery, Loretto Heights College, Denver, Colorado
1979   *City of Lakewood, Colorado, Green Mountain Recreation Center, "Space Frames"

1978   *Church of the Holy Redeemer, Denver, Colorado

1978   Denver Art Museum, Denver, Colorado, "Western States Annual"

1977   *International Wood Sculpture Symposium, Ambelside Park, West Vancouver, B.C. "Standing Wave"

1976   *City of Denver, Colorado, Art in the City, Cherry Creek Drive, "Druid's Drinking Fountain", (Colaboration with Gary Dwyer)

1975   *City of Denver, Art in the City, Denver Convention Center, "Earth Crystal"

1974   Public Art Exhibition, Michigan

1973   American Medical Center, Denver, Colorado, Environmental Sculpture Show

1973   National Gallery of Fine Arts, Washington, D.C., "Community Art's Program"

1973   Colorado Springs Fine Art Center, Colorado Springs, Colorado, "I-25 Alliance"

1972   *Denver Art Museum, Denver, Colorado "Wood Construction"

1972   Denver Art Museum, Denver, Colorado, "Western States Annual"

1971   *State of Colorado, Cherry Creek Resevoir, State Recreation Area, "Shells"

1970   Friends of Contemporary Art, Denver, Colorado, "Symbiosis"

1970   Denver Art Museum, Denver, Colorado University of Denver Faculty Exhibition

1969   *University of Southern Colorado, Pueblo, Colorado, Three Colorado Sculptors, "Wood Construction"

1968   University of Denver, Denver, Colorado, University of Denver Faculty Exhibition

- *Piece now in Permanent Collection*

Professional Activities

International Sculpture Society Member

AIA Associate Member

1982   Board of Governors, Wright Ingraham Institute

1982,81,80,79   Juror, Graduate Architectural Students, University of Colorado, Denver, Colorado

1981,79 Juror, Colorado Council of the Arts and Humanities, Art in Public Places

1981   Juror, Architectural Students, University of Colorado, Boulder, Colorado

1980   Juror, American Institute of Architects Honor Awards Program, North Dakota

1978   Juror, American Society of Landscape, Honor Awards Program, Colorado

Acknowledgements

1983   Alaska State Council on the Arts, Fairbanks International Airport, National Competition First Place

1982   Selected Colorado Representative Artist to Germany InterContinental Alliance, Boulder, Colorado - Munich, Germany

1981   State of Colorado, Colorado Council of the Arts and Humanities, Competition Winner, Art in Public Places Program

1980   Finalist for American Academy in Rome Fellowship

1978   Panelist with I.M. Pei, George Sugarman, William Chaffee and Ira Licht, Art and Architecture, Denver Art Museum

1977   One of three sculptors to represent the United States in Pan American Wood Sculpture Symposium, Vancouver, B.C., Canada

1975   Cherry Creek Shells cited as "Exemplary Design Solution" State of Colorado Colorado Design Assembly

1974   Invited participant in "Man and his World", Vail Symposium, Vail, Colorado

1973   American Institute of Architects Western Region Honor Citation

1972   Represented in "National Community Arts Program"

1972   National Endowment for the Arts, Grant for Art in the City Program, Park People Inc.

1972   Allied Arts Grant

1971-1968   Graduate Teaching Assistantship, University of Denver, Denver, Colorado

Publications

Sculpture International, "Commissions; Sculpture as Regional Symbol", July 1984

Guide to u.s. Architecture: 1940-1980, Ester McCoy, Barbara Goldstein, Art and Architecture Press, 1982.

Architectural Crafts, a Handbook and a Catalog, Bridget Beattie McCarthy, Madrona Publishers, 1982.

Elements of Design, Line, Jack Selleck, Dans Publications, Inc. 1974.

Art Space, "Bob Behrens at Inkfish, Denver April 1981.

Capalano Review, "Robert Behrens, Standing Wave", 1977.

Progressive Architecture, "Sculpture Reflects the City", November, 1977.

L'industria Italiana del Cemento, "Fuori Testo", October 1976.

Architectural Record, "Design for Recreation", November 1975.

Architectural Record, "Ideas, Ingenious, Bold, Playful", August 1975.

National Community Arts Program, 1974.

Interior Design, April 1971.

Design News, June 1966.

Industrial Design, August 1965.